D0934655

Mask and Flippers

The Story of Skin Diving

The Story of Skin Diving

Mask and Flippers

By LLOYD BRIDGES

As told to

BILL BARADA

Illustrated

CHILTON COMPANY · BOOK DIVISION

Publishers

PHILADELPHIA AND NEW YORK

Copyright © 1960 by
LLOYD BRIDGES and BILL BARADA

First Edition
All Rights Reserved

Second Printing, February 1961
Third Printing, May 1961
Fourth Printing, October 1961

34604

Published in Philadelphia by Chilton Company,
and simultaneously in Toronto, Canada,
by Ambassador Books, Ltd.

Library of Congress Catalog Card Number 60–14923

Designed by William E. Lickfield

Manufactured in the United States of America
by Quinn & Boden Company, Inc., Rahway, N. J.

VM
983
B7

Acknowledgments

For additional information and current developments in the world of skin diving, I recommend *The Skin Diver* magazine which is considered the bible of the underwater fraternity. Much of the information contained in this book was obtained from the pages of this magazine, and I wish to extend my specal thanks to Jim Auxier and Chuck Blakesley, owners and editors, for their complete and unselfish co-operation. Address inquiries to: *The Skin Diver*, P.O. Box 128, Lynwood, California.

I also wish to thank the thousands of skin divers, skin diving clubs and councils throughout the world which, through the years, have contributed and shared their knowledge and experience to establish safe diving techniques and procedures. These clubs and councils cover every region of the skin-diving world, and may be contacted through their national organization: The Underwater Society of America, P.O. Box 724, Station A, Champaign, Illinois.

Credit is also to be given to the late Conrad Limbaugh of the Scripps Institution of Oceanography at La Jolla, California. Connie devoted most of his life to underwater sciences and marine biology. His work established new theories and discoveries which enlightened the scientific world about unknown aspects of underwater life. But skin divers best remember Connie for his contributions to the safety of their sport. It was his research and training program for Scripps skin divers that established basic safety rules now generally accepted throughout the world. Connie also was responsible for the research which established standards for pure air and many other innovations, the benefits of which cannot be measured, as they deal with human life.

Connie Limbaugh lost his life in pursuit of his favorite occupation. While exploring an underground river in caves near Marseilles, France, he was caught in a swift current and failed to emerge. The loss of Conrad Limbaugh was a severe blow to both the world of science and skin diving.

Special recognition is also due to Gustav Dalla Valle, a skin diver dedicated to the sport of spearfishing, who has devoted tireless energy and time to the promotion and organization of world-wide underwater spearfishing competitions.

LLOYD BRIDGES

Contents

Bridges' reaction to a new environment.
Why the attraction of underwater.
Sensation of diving.
Vastness of the area and variety of interests available.
Bridges' enjoyment of his work as an actor-diver.
The interest indicated by his fan mail and how the constant stream of questions forced him to increase his knowledge.
This book to tell the story of skin diving as it was learned, the hard way, through experience and experiment by early pioneers. The reader will benefit from Bridges' knowledge, accumulated from the experiences of thousands of divers across the world.

Skin divers in the days of the ancient Greeks.
Fantastic feats of South Sea native pearl divers.
Japanese Ama divers and their bamboo goggles.
Adaptation of Japanese goggles by California lifeguards and the beginning of goggle fishing.
The face mask, flippers, and snorkel, how they came into use and their impact upon skin diving.
Stories and anecdotes illustrating the effect of eye and ear squeeze and how they were overcome.

How cold water affects skin divers and why.
Why skin diving was restricted to temperate waters such as Southern California and the Mediterranean.

The shivering fraternity and their experiments in combatting the cold.

Introduction of dry suits and the "break through" into cold water areas.

Virgin territory opened to exploration. Winter ice diving and the spread of skin diving into the arctic.

Wet suits *vs.* dry suits, advantages and dangers in their use.

Early attempts at underwater breathing and why they failed.

Why it is so difficult to provide a dependable air supply underwater.

Development of helmets, helmet suits and air masks and how they were used.

The first self-contained underwater breathing apparatus (scuba). Oxygen rebreathers, how they worked and why they proved dangerous. Some examples of oxygen poisoning and the results of lessons learned.

The first demand regulator developed in 1866 and how it worked with the probable reasons why it did not become popular.

Modern scuba, how it works and why it has caused an underwater revolution. Advantages of underwater swimming *vs.* the "walk around" system of diving.

Aero-embolism, what it is, how it acts, and what happened to some divers before it was understood.

The bends, what causes them, how to avoid them, and what happens when the rules are broken.

Nitrogen narcosis (diver's drunkenness) and the fatal attraction of the depths.

Dalton's law of partial pressures and Henry's law of the absorption of gases. Ordinary air becomes toxic under pressure at certain depths.

Oil compressors and lipoid pneumonia, and the effect of air contamination.

The abundance of sea life and its prolific reproduction. Conservation and the efficiency of modern methods of harvesting food from the sea.

Underwater spearfishing and its impact upon shallow water sea life. Skin divers are not a threat to fish.

Underwater weapons and techniques in their use. Faulty weapons and some hazards in their use.

Bottom hunting for lobsters, clams and scallops. Some of the unused resources in the sea.

Sharks and skin divers. Some do bite.

Barracuda, moray eels, sting rays, killer whales and octopus. Actual experiments to test their viciousness. Their reputations as killers debunked.

Whales, whale sharks, manta rays and porpoises. They are big but docile creatures of the sea.

Man is the most vicious animal in the world.

Old and new methods compared. Why scuba is faster and cheaper. Impossible accomplishments by skin divers.

Salvage laws and their importance to the skin diver.

Search methods and techniques. Finding a pair of shot guns in a muddy river. Eyeglasses on a sandy bottom.

Sunken treasure and what it takes to get it. Metal detectors, sonar and suction pumps. Most of the gold and jewels are still on the bottom.

Flotation methods, raising heavy objects. Engineering and imagination are required for each operation. No one can tell you how.

Odd job opportunities—Mike Nelson specialties.

As varied as the diver's imagination.

Gold mining, log salvage, sewer pipe installation, criminal investigation, search and recovery.

Salvage diving is similar to a doctor hanging up his shingle. The patients must believe you can cure their ills.

Science underwater; marine biology, geology and archaeology. Conservation for the future and pollution studies.

The skin diver's role in major disasters; floods, ship sinkings, flooded mines, and mobile vehicles underwater. Underwater demolition and underwater warfare.

A new depth to motion pictures within range of moderate budgets. Past methods compared with the present.

Camera work and filming beneath the surface. Difficulties involved with no communication or direction. Limitations for television shows; what can and can't be photographed.

Safety precautions to protect actors with little experience.

Camera work, the pressure-proof case and its importance. Light refraction and the absorption of colors by the water. Steady pictures in a fluid world and the advantages of three dimensions.

Light and visibility; action *vs.* beauty; black and white *vs.* color.

The depth barrier and its effect on breathing mixtures. Future skin divers may explore the continental shelf and examine the bottom at 600 feet.

The abyss and the mystery of great depths. We may conquer space before we reach the depths.

What could be discovered. Mineral deposits, lost cities and civilizations or a graveyard of sunken ships.

Future generations will cruise the sea in submobiles, free from surface turbulence and safe from storms. Skin divers and salvage men will travel to the diving grounds by underwater craft and operations will be conducted from a submerged base. Diving will be unaffected by typhoon or hurricane in the tranquillity of the depths.

No Decompression Time and Depth Table
Navy Standard Decompression Table

Mask and Flippers

Hand Signal System

1. DANGER
Index finger extended
—arm moves in
straight up-and-down
motion (toward sur-
face)—rapidly.

2. UP
Thumb points up.

3. **DOWN**
   Thumb points down.

4. **DIRECTION**
   (FLAT HAND)
   Over reef, around
   reef, under kelp, veer
   left or right.

5. LOOK AT OBJECT
Point with finger.

**6. EVERYONE
ASSEMBLE HERE**
Circle arm overhead.

7. HOLD STILL
One or both arms at 90° angle with fists clenched.

8. HELP ME
Right arm held straight up, palm out —motionless.

9. **EVERYTHING OK**
   Thumb & first finger
   form circle.

10. **AIR SUPPLY
    LOW**
    Closed fist striking
    chest.

**11. ALERT! OTHER
DIVERS IN AREA**
Closed fist makes
circular motion to
side.

12. **ALERT! DANGER-OUS MARINE LIFE**

Open palm makes circular motion to side.

13. **REGARDING QUESTIONS OF DIRECTION, DEPTH, OR TIME**

Point to inside wrist.

14. QUESTION
Free hand palm up.

15. ATTENTION
Bang on tank with rock or other hard object.

Invitation to Adventure

MANY who read this book will wonder how I, a Hollywood actor, came to write a book about the sport of skin diving. The answer lies in a combination of my personal enthusiasm and interest in the sport, the effect of my television role as the fictitious Mike Nelson, and the thousands of letters I receive requesting detailed information about the underwater world. Perhaps, through these pages, I can transmit some small part of the fun and adventure I have discovered beneath the surface of the water.

I have always loved the sea. Its restless surface, changing shoreline, and crashing surf have intrigued my interest and curiosity since I was a small boy. With this interest and curiosity it was only natural that skin diving should be added to my list of sports. But when I first penetrated the surface and experienced the thrill of hunting and exploring in a completely new environment, all other forms of entertainment became tame in comparison. From that first moment underwater, I knew that every spare hour I could squeeze away from mundane duties would be spent submerged. My greatest regret was that the demands of my career left too little time for diving. This is why any skin diver will understand my enthusiasm for the television role of Mike Nelson.

As a fictitious skin-diving character, I have been able to combine my acting career with my favorite activity of skin diving, and it is indeed a fortunate person who can practice the hobby he loves while he is working. Another advantage came with playing the role of Mike Nelson. The work has taken me into some of the world's outstanding diving grounds and has brought me the acquaintance of many skin-diving pioneers. From these men and women I received a composite picture of skin-diving activities as they are actually practiced. From my work on *Sea Hunt*, I learned a great deal of what can and cannot be done while underwater.

To many of my friends the idea of spending hours underwater in the open ocean each week is not only frightening but foolhardy. They share the same apprehensions felt by millions of other unfortunates who are doomed forever to a life on land. As long as these timid individuals are dominated by their nameless fears, they can never know the excitement and thrill of an underwater hunt. However, although these people believe that skin diving is not for them, their letters express an insatiable curiosity about the world beneath the sea and the men who go underwater. Others, less timid, not only express the same curiosity, they ask a constant stream of questions concerning the entire scope of diving. Their letters ask for detailed information about how to get started in skin diving; they want answers to everything from technical diving problems to the best defense against sharks.

Through the mysterious alchemy of motion pictures, I found myself not only acting the part of Mike Nelson on the screen, but living it off stage as well. This led to a problem. As the imaginary Mike Nelson, I am expected to have a detailed knowledge of every phase of skin diving. I am also expected to participate in every major diving activity since the sport began. Since, in a single lifetime, no individual could possibly embrace such a vast field in his own person, I have tried to do the next best thing and arm myself with whatever knowledge is available.

The information and adventures described in this book are not only my personal observations and experiences but the accumulated knowledge and experience of thousands of skin divers throughout the world. This accumulation of knowledge has made Mike Nelson possible. It has also made it possible for me to take you back to the days when skin diving first began and safety rules were unknown. In this manner we can live again when the sea was even more of a mystery and accompany the Mike Nelsons of history as they painfully learned the laws of diving, the hard way, through experience.

One of the questions I am most often asked is why skin diving has such an attraction for me. The questioners want to know what there is underwater to cause thousands of skin divers to drive hundreds of miles just to explore the bottom of some lake or abandoned rock quarry. The answer, I am sure, lies in the sensations derived from just being underwater. It is like nothing else I have ever experienced. Once we have mastered our equipment and overcome our initial apprehension, we feel a sense of freedom impossible to describe. It is like being able to fly without wings. As in a dream, we hang suspended over a submerged world, our weight supported by the water. Everything is below us and we move over a panorama of seascapes every bit as spectacular and changing as anything above the surface. The submarine terrain offers a never-ending variety. We float over grassy plains stretching as far as the eye can see, the fields undulating gently with the passing swells as if pushed by a changing breeze. Great sandy deserts rivaling the Sahara pass beneath us, their surface riffled into geometric patterns by the swirling water. We cruise effortlessly over submerged mountains or drift down the face of sheer rock cliffs. In mid-flight, we can pause to explore and examine nooks and crevices on the face of a precipice while below us yawns a bottomless abyss.

Details of almost any object underwater can be studied at close quarters. Within our depth range, the bottoms of sheer canyons and the tips of fragile pinnacles are as accessible as a shallow, sandy floor. We only need to point ourselves in their direction and kick our flippers. In slow motion, we fly over all obstructions directly to our goal. And we can hover there until our curiosity is satisfied.

But probably the greatest attraction is a sense of well-being.

3

Even the weight of the atmosphere is left behind and our muscles, accustomed to supporting our weight against the tremendous pull of gravity, are relieved of this load. Underwater we can relax completely and the weightlessness gives us a feeling of exhilaration. We can perform fantastic feats of physical strength which, on the surface, would be possible only to a superman. We can do a handstand on the tip of one finger, leap over a hundred feet in a single bound, and lift tremendous weights with ease. We no longer feel clumsy and, like the fish which are the birds of this world, we can weave our way through submarine forests and jungles without disturbing their pattern. We feel no sense of pressure and no discomfort. With modern cold water suits, even in ice water we feel as though swimming in a warm bath, and our breathing equipment adjusts automatically to changing pressure. We are as free as a feather floating in a breeze.

In deep water, when sight of both the surface and the bottom are lost, we have no sense of direction. Like spacemen of the sea floating in a vacuum, there is no up or down and no feel of gravity. We can only tell in what direction we are headed by our exhaled bubbles as they flash and sparkle like dancing quicksilver on their way to the surface. It is here, in an airless void without top or bottom, that the skin diver feels the vastness of the water world with its unexplored miles leading down into the abysmal depths. Sometimes, in deep water, we feel a dangerous intoxication caused from breathing air under great pressure. In this state we occasionally feel an irresistible urge to descend deeper and deeper into areas where no man has been before. Thus enraptured, some divers have succumbed to the fascination of the depths and continued down, never to be seen again. But this is deep water sickness and not to be feared in the shallows. The fatal attraction of shallow water is in the beauty of its colorful submarine gardens and the lure of its unexplored caverns. Here hours pass like minutes and no day is

4

long enough to satisfy our curiosity. The addiction to skin diving is not fatal but the disease is hard to cure.

Scientists tell us that all life originated in the sea and, in some ancient ocean, our ancestors fought for survival with other denizens of the deep. Perhaps this accounts for our quick adaptation to the fluid world and our apprehension toward its inhabitants. Always when submerged, we are aware of trespassing in a world inhabited by strange creatures whose appetites are unknown to us. We are becoming acquainted with the animals of the sea, but we are strangers and have much to learn. In the ocean, we may encounter almost any of its grotesque forms of life from microscopic organisms almost invisible to the naked eye, to giant sperm whales measuring over 60 feet in length. Practically all forms, from the graceful angelfish to the deadly, marauding shark, inhabit the same shallow coastal waters visited by the skin diver. But even in the sea, we have learned that man is the aggressor and far more dangerous to sea denizens than they are to him. Swimming with the monsters of the sea is much safer than driving in modern traffic and the small element of danger that does exist only adds zest to the adventure.

The playground of the skin diver offers an infinite variety of interests to satisfy almost every taste. Whether it is probing the beauties of some secluded mountain lake or accepting the challenge of the ocean's depths, the possibilities for adventure are endless. Three fourths of the world's surface is covered by water and most of it is unexplored. Some day, no doubt, men will solve the problems of tremendous pressure and descend into the abyss. But right now, with modern diving equipment, the shallow water bordering our lakes, rivers and continents is accessible for exploration. This is a tremendous area with the most prolific abundance of sea life and colorful vegetation known to man. We can work in the surge and turbulence of ocean swells, in the currents of swift-flowing rivers and over soft, muddy bottoms of lakes with

5

ease where heavy, helmet equipment is cumbersome and difficult to handle. Our lightweight, inexpensive equipment is so mobile that hitherto inaccessible regions can now be probed. Our range of salvage and recovery operations is from the highest mountain lake to the deepest jungle river. We can transport our equipment with equal ease by horse, boat, auto, or plane and wherever there is transportation, skin divers can work.

Throughout the ages of history, fortunes in gold and silver and jewels have gone to the bottom. The treasures of entire kingdoms still lie unrecovered on the floors of all the seas. Much of this lies in shallow water areas too risky for expensive expeditions but within easy range of the skin diver. With the freedom of our light equipment and working from small boats, we can hunt in the shallow, turbulent waters of a jagged reef or probe beyond the breakers of a rocky headland. With luck and perseverance, any skin diver may uncover the remains of an ancient treasure.

Opportunities for serious underwater occupations are limited only by the imagination and initiative of the individual diver. We can engage in shell and rock collecting or underwater gold mining. The scientific-minded can increase our knowledge through marine biology and oceanography or they can help tap the resources of the sea through archeology and geology. We are even called upon to play detective and engage in underwater search and recovery or investigations. And some are recording the beauties beneath the surface through underwater photography and motion pictures. Few areas in recent times have offered the challenge and opportunities to the average person that are now opening to the skin diver. But he must be skilled in use of underwater tools and familiar with his new environment.

Like any other skill, skin diving must be learned before it can be enjoyed. Among the many tests a skin diver must pass before he is competent underwater is one which will confront him again and again as he is led into new and untried situa-

6

tions. This test has nothing to do with physical health and stamina, although these are very important. Neither does it draw upon your skill and ability as a swimmer. It is the personal struggle within yourself to overcome the instinctive fear of the unknown. Nature has wisely provided us with a built-in warning system through which we are alerted to danger. In strange and unknown surroundings, this warning system is tuned to a high pitch and we are keenly aware of fear and apprehension that can easily turn to panic. And panic underwater can be far more serious than in most other situations.

For the novice diver, unfamiliar with his equipment and cautiously feeling his way into a world where he knows he doesn't belong, panic is an ever-present possibility. Fortunately, as our skill improves and we become familiar with our surroundings, apprehension disappears. Only then do we feel the freedom and relaxation of the fluid world. But then a new situation is encountered, the warning system is alerted, and we must pass the test again.

The wise beginner takes full advantage of the knowledge available. Through competent instruction and by following guideposts and techniques learned from lessons of the past, he can soon achieve the skill and confidence necessary for full enjoyment of skin diving.

Basic Equipment and the First Skin Divers

F ROM the letters I receive it is clear that, in the popular conception, skin diving is practiced entirely with the aid of breathing apparatus. It is also clear that too many people have been given the impression it is far safer to take breathing equipment underwater than to dive and hold their breath. Nothing could be farther from the truth. Yet the belief that modern breathing equipment has eliminated all need for safety precautions or instruction has been so firmly implanted in people's minds by unscrupulous promoters that it has caused far too many deaths. In fact, a number of cases are on record where people who couldn't even swim have tried diving with a tank.

In one case I was an unwilling witness to such an unnecessary tragedy. One which certainly could and should have been prevented had the circumstances been known earlier, or if the victim had been properly advised when he purchased his equipment.

A companion and I were skin diving off Point Dume in Southern California when it happened. We were about a hundred yards from shore, snorkeling on the surface, when we heard a terrific shouting from spectators on the beach. They were waving and pointing to a clump of exposed rocks between us and the shore. I looked in that direction and was horrified to see the figure of a skin diver clinging desperately to the rocks, and being pounded by the surf. Each time a wave came crashing into the rocks he and the heavy tank strapped to his back would disappear under a boiling mass of white water. He was obviously in trouble and couldn't hold his precarious grip much longer.

I swam in his direction as fast as my flippers would take me. A heavy surface kelp bed between me and the diver made it necessary to swim underwater until I cleared it. When my head broke the surface past the kelp, the skin diver was gone. Nothing but waves and rocks met my vision.

Around the exposed rocks my companion and I timed our dives between sets of breakers. We had to grope blindly over the rocky bottom as the turbulence of the water made it too murky to see anything. If a breaker came through while we were under, we held ourselves against the boil and surge by clinging tight to the rocks. It took five minutes of this kind of diving before we finally found the body and towed him to shore.

On the beach a lifeguard ambulance was waiting with an inhalator and they brought him around with artificial respiration. Someone asked him what had happened to make him cling to the exposed rocks in the surf. The man answered that he had run out of air and was trying to get back to shore. I told him it would have been better to jettison his tank. Then he could swim and tow it to shore. He looked at me and said, "But—I can't swim." He had been reading books about how easy it was to become a man-fish. An unscrupulous salesman had told him the breathing apparatus was foolproof and that even little kids could start right out with it.

The purpose of this story is not to discourage anyone from using breathing apparatus, except those who are unable to swim. The salesman who sold this man his equipment was right in one respect. Modern breathing equipment is as foolproof as a modern automobile. But, like an automobile, it isn't safe until you learn how to drive. And in the case of breathing underwater, learning how means learning what you can do and what you cannot do with all of your equipment. It means learning to handle yourself both underwater and

9

on the surface when something goes wrong. It also means learning what changing air pressure can do to your body if you don't obey the rules. These rules can be learned from reading books such as this one, but skin diving experts almost universally agree that the best and safest way is to start with simple basic equipment and dive while holding your breath. Become acquainted with the underwater world and familiar with your environment before trying to become a man-fish.

Most people, when it is suggested they hold their breath to skin dive, feel that the attempt would be hopeless. They believe they can't hold their breath long enough or that they are not good enough swimmers. Usually these people are thinking of the exertion required in ordinary swimming and believe that skin diving demands the same effort. It doesn't. Not with modern swimming aids such as mask, flippers and snorkel. If this were not true, there would probably be no greater number of skin divers today than there were in the early days of the sport. If mask and flippers had not been developed, modern breathing equipment would be useless and skin diving would still be in much the same stage of advancement it was in in biblical days of the ancient Greeks and Romans. Modern masks, flippers and snorkels take the effort out of swimming and diving and they make an average person the equal or better than these "iron men" of the past.

We like to think of skin diving as a modern innovation and that we are the first to explore the mysteries of the sea. Skin diving is modern only in the sense that new equipment has brought the underwater world within the reach of almost everyone. But there were others before us. As far back in history as our records go, we find evidence of ancient divers who worked beneath the surface. As long ago as 750 years before Christ, Greek skin divers worked to depths of 100 feet on the floor of the Mediterranean. Without mask, flippers, goggles, or bathing suit, these ancestors of our modern skin divers collected sponges and mollusks on the ocean floor.

The use of divers in warfare also is not new. Legends of those same ancient times tell of heroic underwater warriors who routed or captured entire enemy fleets, sometimes single-handed. Gun powder and explosives were unknown and battles were won or lost through hand-to-hand combat. Under these conditions, skin divers could work at close range, cutting anchor cables, chopping holes in the bottoms of boats, and generally causing confusion among enemy shipping. I like to imagine what it would be like if one of those legendary skin divers could come to life and tell us in his own words of one of his famous exploits.

Let's listen while a young Greek sponge diver of the year 750 B.C. tells how he happened to establish a precedent that elevated divers to a highly respected position in his society.

"Before the event occurred I was a lowly sponge diver living on the shore of the Mediterranean in the prosperous city of Byzantium. Although I was the strongest swimmer and could go deeper than any other diver, my pay was poor and my status was little better than a common slave. I envied the warriors of our army who, when not seeking glory in battle, were toasted and feted by the populace. But they were selected by the Emperor and there was little chance for me, a common diver, to hope for a hero's death.

"At sunset of the seventh day, after the army had left Byzantium to do battle in distant fields, the city was electrified by the terrifying cry of 'raiders.' I heard the cry and hurried to the beach. In my mind was the hope that I could help in preparations for defense. I thought that, with the army away, even a sponge diver might get into the fighting.

"Everywhere along the way the streets were blocked by a confusion of horses, ox carts, and hand carts as the people hastily prepared to flee from danger. When I finally reached the beach I saw the raiders. Eleven Persian warships were anchored across the entrance to the bay. They were only a few hundred yards from shore, so close I could hear their voices and the clanking of their armor. Each ship was swarm-

11

ing with warriors eagerly anticipating the plunder of our help-less city. At the parapets by the docks, only a few hundred palace regulars prepared to meet the onslaught.

"My offer of assistance met nothing but derision. A soldier asked if I planned to fight the entire Persian army single-handed. I answered that at least it would be a hero's death, not that of a cowardly jackal hiding in the bush. My answer must have touched the Captain. He explained that his small force only hoped to obtain delay. The Persians, if unaware Byzantium was defenseless, would wait until daylight to at-tack. After the people had left the city, his force would fol-low to protect them from pursuit. There was bitterness in the Captain's voice as he told me he could fight one ship at a time. But he said only a fool would stand against all eleven of them at once. It was then that the idea struck me that was to change the course of history. I told the Captain of my plan and he agreed to let me try.

"Early that night, in bright moonlight, I stripped off my clothes and slipped into the black water. In my teeth was a sharp knife and on my arm was a long coil of strong rope. One end of the rope was attached to the dock and as I swam, I let the coil play out into the water. If my plan was to suc-ceed, it was important to swim very quietly without making a splash to attract the attention of the Persians. To make sure of this, I swam the entire distance underwater. I swam as far as I could while holding my breath, surfaced only long enough to replenish the air in my lungs, then submerged and continued underwater.

"I reached the first ship undetected and located its anchor line. I dived to the bottom and cut it free from the anchor. Then, still working underwater, I tied my rope from shore to the loose end of the anchor rope. The ship was now tied to the docks of Byzantium instead of being safely anchored to the bottom. Swimming quietly in the same manner as be-fore, I returned to shore.

"The captain and the guards were waiting and, with all

12

of us on the rope, we began pulling the ship toward the dock. As it slowly gained momentum, we heard the shouts of a sentry on board. Soon other shouts joined the sentry's and were followed by a confused clattering and banging inside the ship. But the ship touched the dock and we swarmed aboard before the surprised Persians knew what was happening. Their terrified screams were quickly stilled as we easily cut them to pieces.

"Once again I took the coil of rope and headed back into the sea. By this time pandemonium had broken out aboard the other ships. Even so, by working underwater, I was able to attach the rope to a second ship and return to shore unobserved. As the second ship left the fleet on its slow journey to the dock, the cries and shouts of its warriors filled the air. Their ship, seemingly moved by an invisible power, headed straight to shore as if controlled by magic. As the ship drew close the Persians' terror turned to panic. In frantic efforts to escape this unseen power, many jumped into the water. We swarmed aboard and the shrieks of dying Persians put fear into the hearts of the remaining warriors. By the time the fight was over the other ships had pulled anchor and were heading out to sea.

"The Emperor learned how a lowly sponge diver had saved Byzantium and his gratitude knew no bounds. I was granted land, money, and slaves to fit my new position as captain of the first battalion of underwater warriors."

An incident very similar to this actually occurred in those ancient times. It and other accounts of underwater warfare appear in legends throughout ancient history. But the discovery of gun powder ended the usefulness of skin divers in warfare until they were again called into service during World War II. Still, throughout the ages, these unequipped "iron men" of the past continued to demonstrate an amazing ability to work beneath the surface.

Even today, native pearl divers in the South Pacific spurn the use of modern equipment in favor of primitive methods.

13

I have witnessed underwater feats by these native divers that equal anything accomplished in the past. Trained from early childhood for a life of skin diving, many of them work at depths of 130 feet and stay under for periods up to five minutes on each dive. Their technique is simple. With a heavy rock held in their arms, they simply drop into the water and let the rock take them to the bottom. A basket or net tied to the end of a rope is quickly filled with pearl shells. Then the diver ascends, climbs into his outrigger, and pulls his catch to the surface. This process is repeated time after time throughout a day's diving.

Once, in the Philippines, I was watching a group of native divers and considered introducing them to modern breathing equipment. But, after thinking it over, I realized the complications such equipment might bring into their simple lives. Actually, breathing equipment would be of little benefit to them. A single tank of air at the depths they work would only last about fifteen minutes. A double tank or a hose and compressor would make them subject to the bends and other pressure problems which they couldn't cope with. Also, even if they could be taught to use the equipment safely, the increase in their production would hardly pay for the extra expense. It was quite a shock to realize that primitive diving methods, without equipment of any kind, is sometimes more effective than modern inventions. Some of us tried to equal the performance of these divers by using mask and flippers and holding our breath. None of us could reach the depth the native pearl divers were working.

But these are examples of the "iron men" of skin diving and the ability and stamina required are far beyond the reach of the average person. Without the aid of basic equipment, skin diving would still be limited to the "iron men" of the sea instead of being a pastime for millions of enthusiasts.

It was a simple pair of goggles that started skin diving

14

as a sport. They originated with the women Ama divers of Japan who harvest the special seaweed from which agar-agar is made. This short, brown weed is found growing on the surface of submerged rocks along many shallow coast lines. But it took the frugal Japanese to harvest and convert it into the gelatinous substance from which many drugs are made. Today your corner drugstore is selling many products containing agar-agar harvested by the Amas of Japan. These same goggles, carved from bamboo, shell, or even wood, found their way to the Mediterranean and to the coast of Southern California. But it took the idle hours and shortage of ready cash in the big depression of the 1930s to send Americans underwater after food. Then the beachniks of those jobless years found an underwater bonanza through the use of simple Japanese goggles.

The goggles took hours of sanding and filing before they fitted the contours of the individual diver's face and formed a watertight seal. But when this was accomplished an air space was created between the swimmer's eyes and the water and, for the first time, blurred vision was eliminated. Water has only one third the light refraction of air and when our eyes are in direct contact with water, they are unable to correct for the difference. By fixing an air space over our eyes while we are underwater, our eyes can function normally and we can see almost as clearly as on the surface.

With the vision supplied by goggles, a handful of unemployed lifeguards and swimmers found a bountiful larder beyond the breakers of Southern California. Hiding in crevices of submerged reefs off Palos Verdes, La Jolla and Laguna Beach, they found luscious abalone, lobsters and scallops, which the divers either ate themselves or traded for less exotic foods. Among these same reefs lived a prolific abundance of fish which, to the skin diver's surprise, could be approached very closely by swimming underwater. A crude pole spear was developed and the sport of goggle fishing began. Word

15

of their exploits spread and, with typical American enthusiasm for a sport that promised adventure, more and more goggle fishermen joined the ranks of underwater hunters.

From these first pioneers came many of the techniques and safety rules which are still in use today. One of the early lessons was that an "eye squeeze" could be caused by the air space inside the goggles and this led directly to development of the face mask.

One of my friends experienced this "squeeze" and I have his own story of how it happened. His story also illustrates a few of the difficulties encountered while diving without equipment and the danger of learning safety the hard way, through experience. Here is his story:

"We were working Abalone Cove off Palos Verdes. The one where the point drops right off into deep water. We liked this point for that reason. It was pretty tough getting in and out over the rocks through the breakers when we didn't have flippers. If we went in at a shallow, protected cove, it took so long to get out for the diving that we 'froze out' before we made it. In deep water, the trick was to time our entrance with the swells and let the backwash take us out over the rocks. If a guy missed his timing, he could get cut up pretty badly. Those rocks are sharp.

"I used an old tire tube to hold my sack on the surface and, if I used it right, the tube was a big help in getting in and out through the breakers. I had an old pole spear made out of a broom handle and a frog gig and I wore a pair of tennis shoes to keep my feet from getting cut on the rocks. By keeping the shoes on while I was in the water I was sure to have them no matter where I came out. The only other thing I carried was an abalone iron tied to my wrist with a heavy cord. The iron was for prying abalone off the rocks while I was diving. These mollusks have a powerful suction and can stick so tight on a rock it takes a strong iron like a crowbar to pry them loose.

"With my goggles on my forehead, I worked my way over

16

the rocks out to the point, and climbed down into the water up to my waist. Each time a swell came in, I had to brace myself and hang onto the rocks to keep from being washed away. The surge piled water high up on the rocks, then the backwash sucked it back like a millrace. If we got caught in close, before a swell came in, the surge would make mincemeat of us on the barnacles. When a big swell came in against the rocks, I lay on the tube and rode the backwash out beyond the breaker line. Out there I could relax. If the surge pushed me around I just floated over the bottom without getting cut up.

"I had about ten abalone and three or four lobsters in my sack when the accident happened. Usually we only worked about fifteen or twenty feet deep because there was plenty of stuff without going any deeper. But this time I was working the edge of a ledge over a deep cut in the rocks when I saw the feelers of a big lobster sticking out of a crack and I went after him. I grabbed him but he broke away and I followed him toward the bottom. It was deeper than I had ever been before and I noticed a funny pressure on my eyes. As I reached for the bug a light flashed across my eyes and I felt a blinding pain. My vision was a little blurred but I could see enough to make my way back to the surface.

"When my buddies saw my eyes they said I looked like I had been hit with a baseball bat. My eyes were black and blue and for a couple of weeks I had an awful time explaining those shiners.

"But my troubles that day weren't over. I still had to make it through the surf to get back to shore. The way we did it was to catch a swell and ride it into the rocks. Just before we touched, we put our hands and feet ahead of us to keep our bodies from getting skinned up. If we missed our grip, we kicked back and waited for the next one. This time I missed my grip and, when I kicked away, the abalone iron dangling from my wrist caught in the rocks. I couldn't get it loose and I couldn't get the cord off my wrist. The back-

17

wash pummeled me over the rocks like a punching bag. I was still hanging by my wrist when the next swell came in. Then the surge of tons of water banged me in the opposite direction. When the cord on the iron finally broke, I was half drowned and my body was a mass of bruises and cuts. Those two lessons grounded me for a month. But I learned never to tie anything to me that I couldn't get loose, and that goggles were no good in deep water."

The "eye squeeze," or any other type of squeeze experienced underwater, is caused by the difference in pressure between the air inside a flexible container and the surrounding water. In deep water, the pressure increases and the squeeze becomes greater as the air inside the container is compressed. A balloon full of air on the surface will be compressed to one half its size at 33 feet, one third its size at 66 feet and one fourth its size at 99 feet. This is Boyle's law of compressed gases which is extremely important to the use and functioning of breathing apparatus and is discussed in detail in another chapter. In the case of my friend's eye squeeze, the goggles could not contract sufficiently to balance the increased pressure. The result was that his eyes were squeezed into the goggles as the pressure of the water increased.

This same type of squeeze causes ear pain when we fail to equalize pressures. We have an air space in our inner ear, behind the eardrum. If, when we dive, this air space remains at surface pressure, the water squeezes our eardrums inward and we feel a sharp pain. Fortunately, nature has provided us with the means to equalize the pressure in this space and eliminate the pain. We have a tiny tube, called the Eustachian tube, leading from our throat to the space in the inner ear. Through this tube, air from our lungs can be admitted behind the eardrum and the squeeze prevented. As long as the air pressure inside a container is equal to that of the surrounding water, the container holds its shape and no squeeze occurs. Unless we have a head cold or similar obstruction to the Eustachian tube, it can be trained to open readily and admit air behind our eardrums. The air inside our lungs will always be compressed to a pressure equal to that of the surrounding water. The walls of our chest are flexible and contract in the same manner as the balloon.

To equalize pressure in your ears or in your sinus cavities, it helps to swallow, work your jaws, or hold your nose and blow. But if the pain persists, don't go any deeper. Hundreds of skin divers with ruptured eardrums will tell you what might happen if you do. And using ear plugs won't keep the water pressure off your ears. In fact, using them can cause more trouble than diving with a head cold. Ear plugs create an air space in the ear canal which is subject to a squeeze. This is another lesson that was learned the hard way and an experience of my own will illustrate the danger.

I had been using ear plugs for a few months. They were of soft, flexible rubber and formed an efficient seal which prevented any water from entering my ears. They worked fine until one day, when the water was exceptionally clear, I spotted a cluster of large abalone in a crevice about ten feet below my usual depth. I took several deep breaths to fill my lungs with fresh air, then headed for the bottom. To my surprise, the extra depth didn't bother me and I reached the abalone without any trouble. But when I strained to pry one off the rocks, I heard a hiss in my right ear that sounded like a high pressure air leak. Then I felt as though a miniature explosion had hit me in the head and this was followed by a sharp pain inside my ear. The bottom began to spin and tilt and when I looked around me, things were spinning in all directions. It was like swimming inside a giant whirlpool.

I started for the surface, then realized I didn't know where it was. My equilibrium was gone and things were spinning at such crazy angles I couldn't tell down from up. To make things worse, a nausea worse than seasickness threatened my dwindling air reserve. In near panic I watched the bottom swing and roll around me, hoping for some clue that would lead me to the surface. I was running out of gas and couldn't hold my breath much longer.

Finally, in desperation, I exhaled some air bubbles. And in dismay, I watched them drift away in a horizontal circle. In my topsy-turvy condition, even the kelp was growing sideways instead of toward the surface. That thought proved to be my salvation. I forced myself to follow the kelp even though it appeared to extend horizontally in an ever curving circle.

The surface was a welcome sight but it was tilted at a crazy angle. Swimming toward it was like swimming toward the side of an aquarium. Even when my head broke through and I could get a breath of air, my troubles weren't over. It looked as if I was swimming near the center of the whirlpool and in all directions the water slanted up and away at a steep angle. At the top of the wall of water floated my tube and sack. But reaching them proved almost too much of a struggle. My arms and legs refused to co-ordinate and the water appeared too steep.

My companions finally saw me floundering on the surface and towed me to my tube. But I had to close my eyes to keep from falling off. Every time I looked around, the water started spinning and I overturned the tube. We finally reached the beach and the safety of dry land but the vertigo was still with me. For several days I couldn't walk without falling.

An ear doctor removed the ear plug and explained what had happened. The squeeze of water pressure had shot the ear plug into my ear like a pellet from an air gun. The sudden shock had ruptured my eardrum and the dizziness and nausea were caused by cold water entering the middle ear. Fortunately, the depth at which it happened was only thirty feet and the damage to my eardrum wasn't permanent. Three weeks later I was out skin diving again, but the ear plugs were at home stored with relics of the past.

Nature has provided us with the means to equalize pressures in our ears and sinus cavities but the goggles posed a problem. Until eye equeeze was eliminated we were doomed to shallow water. Some method had to be developed which would pressurize the air space over our eyes when we were underwater. One method which proved partially successful was the attachment of rubber balls and tubing to the goggles. As we descended, the balls compressed and forced air into the goggles. But the balls continually caught on kelp or rocks and caused the goggles to leak. Sometimes just turning our heads was enough to pull them loose.

Then, somewhere, an ingenious skin diver thought of enclosing our nose inside the glass with our eyes and the first face mask made its appearance. This proved the perfect answer to our problem. Simply exhaling through our nose pressurized the mask. But equally important, the single pane of glass eliminated the double vision sometimes encountered with the goggles. We had better vision, more comfort, and no eye squeeze at any depth.

Modern face masks come in a variety of shapes, sizes and designs to give a perfect seal on any facial contour. Among them are compensator masks for deep diving which permit you to hold your nose and force rapid clearing of your ears. Also available are self-purging masks which automatically clear themselves of any water when you exhale through your nose. However, any face mask can be cleared of water without rising to the surface. The purging process requires a little practice but is not difficult to learn.

To clear a mask we take advantage of the fact that underwater air always rises toward the surface. To fill a submerged container with air, we simply turn it upside down and pour air in underneath. Air is trapped in the container and water is forced out of the opening in the bottom. The glass of a mask is the bottom of the container. We turn the mask upside down by looking up at the surface. Air is poured into the mask through our nose and any water inside the mask is forced out of the opening around our face. The process is speeded up by holding the lowest portion of the mask away from our face as we exhale. But be sure to exhale continually while the mask is held open. If you stop before it is sealed, the mask will immediately fill with water through the opening.

With a good face mask, properly fitted to give a perfect, airtight seal, we can see underwater as clearly as we can see in the air; provided the water is clear. No water enters our nose or eyes to cause the blurred vision or blindness common to ordinary swimming. And, with our nose encased in air, the strangling feeling, so objectionable to many people, is overcome. The increased vision afforded by face masks encouraged more recruits to swell the ranks of underwater explorers. But it was the flipper which gave skin diving its greatest impetus.

The widespread popularity flippers enjoy today makes it difficult to realize that, at one time, no manufacturer would consider adding them to his line and no sporting goods store would put them on display. Lifeguards and swimming instructors turned them down and it was many years before even skin divers believed in their usefulness. If it hadn't been for the conviction of one man, encouraged by the American system of private enterprise, we might still be struggling along without the aid of flippers.

In the 1930s, Owen Churchill was swimming with South Sea natives and was amazed at the increased efficiency they obtained simply by wearing palm fronds strapped to their feet while in the water. Intrigued by the innovation, he tried the trick himself and was surprised to find that the ease and speed of his swimming were greatly increased. Owen returned to California with the idea and, after a series of tests, the first swim fins were perfected and patented. But no manufacturer or sporting goods distributor would undertake their sale. He was considered a crazy inventor and his swim fins just another wild idea that no one would ever buy. In disgust, Owen finally set up a factory and began making the flippers himself. At first their sale was so slow that it appeared his critics were right. Nobody would be bothered with rubber paddles on his feet. Then skin divers discovered his flippers and recognized their value. Each customer became a salesman and their use began to spread. Today flippers are in common use throughout the world for every type of swimming. Their use has made swimmers of nonswimmers. They made Underwater Demolition Teams possible during World War II. But most of all, they brought the beauty, mystery and excitement of the underwater world within the reach of millions of average swimmers.

An old-timer in West Coast skin diving, accustomed to diving without flippers, tells us what happened when he tried them for the first time.

"I tried my first pair of flippers during a dive at Laguna Beach. I didn't know that my companion had purchased a pair and he sneaked into the water with them while I was busy with something else. Then, as I struggled through the water toward the reef, he put on a display of swimming ability that baffled me completely. With both hands above his head, he cut through the water as if driven by a propeller. Then, with his hands still in the air, he stopped and treaded water shoulder high. I was pushing with all my power to stay even with him, using the old method of both hands combined with a frog-like kick. But, in spite of my best efforts, he easily swam circles around me. When we finally arrived at the reef, I was puffing like a steam engine and my companion was breathing easily. It was only after I threatened him with mayhem that he relented and showed me the reason for his new-found power. I borrowed his strange looking rubber feet and tried my first flippered dive.

"It is easy to imagine what happened. I was used to the terrific struggle of diving to the bottom in bare feet. A pole spear held in one hand and an abalone iron in the other made the process a little like climbing up the side of a sandy cliff. With each stroke we would seem to gain one and lose two in trying to reach the bottom. With the flippers on, I jacknifed, kicked my feet, and almost banged my head into the rocks before I managed to stop. Even more important, I found that the spear and abalone iron were no longer any hindrance. The flippers eliminated the need for arms and hands in swimming and these were free for other uses. I could propel myself easily over the bottom with less effort than ever before. Then, back on the surface, I found that I could rest and regain my breath far more quickly than in the past. Needless to say, after this experience, my own pair of swim fins accompanied me on every dive."

Today's novice skin diver is confronted with flippers in such a variety of shapes and sizes that selection can be as confusing as selecting an automobile. However, there are a few guides which, if followed, will help determine the size and type best suited to a particular individual.

The proper blade size of a pair of flippers should fit the power developed by an individual's legs. Flippers too large for a person's legs will tire him and cause cramps, without giving the speed or endurance he should have. A pair of flippers ten feet long would give terrific power to the man who could kick them. Usually it is best to start with small-size flippers and graduate to the larger, heavier type after considerable practice. More attention should be given to comfort than to design, as it is difficult to apply full power to a pair of flippers that hurt your feet. But durability is important and depends almost entirely upon the quality and workmanship in the materials used. But whatever flippers are selected, they take the work out of swimming and give propulsion through the water equal to that of an expert swimmer.

The perfecting of flippers left only one additional problem to be solved before skin diving became almost as simple as swimming in a pool. This problem concerned breathing on the surface while our face is in the water.

The skin diver who invented the first snorkel must have

conceived the idea while watching porpoises or whales. These are air-breathing mammals but nature wisely placed their noses on top of their heads so they can breathe while their eyes are underwater. A snorkel is a mechanical means by which a skin diver accomplishes the same thing. The name is derived from the German *schnorkel* submarine which drew air through a tube reaching to the surface while it was submerged. The skin diver's snorkel is a tube with a mouthpiece on one end. The tube is bent into a "U" shape and when the mouthpiece is in place, the opposite end of the tube is above the surface. With a snorkel in his mouth, a diver can float motionless face down on the surface and continue to breathe. It is no longer necessary to tread water with our heads above the surface while we gasp for air. All effort is removed and we can keep an eye on the world beneath us at all times. The advantage of this function is best appreciated when a shark approaches or we are stalked by a curious sea lion. In such a situation we can keep a sharp eye on the creatures until their intentions are determined.

Selection of a snorkel is a matter of individual preference. Most experts recommend one that is flexible because it has less chance of snagging or catching in weeds and rocks. Also, no expert of my acquaintance uses a snorkel with a ping-pong ball attachment. An open snorkel in your mouth will not fill your lungs with water when you dive. Air in our mouth is pressurized and holds the water out. A snorkel full of water on the surface can be easily cleared by blowing sharply through our mouth.

The mask, flippers, and snorkel are the three items of basic equipment which opened the way for a mass invasion of the underwater world. With these aids, most people's natural fear of water disappears. The mask lets them see what is underneath them and no water enters the nose or eyes. The flippers push them through the water with very little exertion. And the snorkel answers the problem of breathing while they swim. With only the small investment required for this equipment and a little practice in its use, almost anyone can explore the world of shallow water.

It is here that we learn to handle ourselves and our equipment and find how much there is for us to see and do. By holding our breath for a fraction of a minute, we can hunt fish, shellfish, and lobsters. Or the same short period gives us time to take underwater photographs, collect rare shells and semiprecious stones, or just enjoy the beauty of the sea. But never underestimate the potential of simple basic equipment. Even today, with an abundance of breathing equipment to choose from, over half of all skin diving is practiced by divers who hold their breath.

~~3~~

The Cold Water Barrier

THE ease of diving with mask, flippers, and snorkel let us venture farther and deeper under the sea. But our explorations were still confined to warm waters such as southern California, Florida and the Mediterranean. The tremendous underwater areas bordering the continents of the northern hemisphere were covered by a barrier of water too cold for skin divers to penetrate. Without effective protection against the cold, over half of the underwater world would forever remain a mystery. Even in temperate water, as warm as 60 degrees, underwater time was limited and a "freeze-out" came too soon. For all except a handful who braved the winter cold, skin diving was restricted to a brief span of balmy summer weather, and then only for short periods of immersion. More time was spent shivering and shaking around a fire on the beach than in the water.

A skin diver is affected by cold water far more readily than a swimmer. When swimming we are exercising constantly and burn energy which helps to maintain body heat. While skin diving we move through the water with the least possible exertion to conserve our energy for the time we are submerged. When we rest motionless on the surface, body heat is carried away at a terrific rate, and we quickly become chilled. In addition, water near the bottom is almost always colder than surface temperatures and, while exposed to this colder temperature, we are under pressure and holding our breath. The pressure seems to drive the cold deep into our bodies, and holding our breath depletes our blood of oxygen, which adds to the reduction of its temperature.

Water is an almost perfect cooling agent and absorbs heat so rapidly that, in extremely cold water, body temperature is quickly reduced to a dangerous level. An example of this is seen in the fact that, dressed in warm clothing, men can live and work when air temperature is 60 degrees below zero. But dressed in the same clothing, a ten minute immersion in ice water can be fatal. Just as water always flows downhill, heat flows from a warmer object to a colder one until the temperatures are equal. The greater the difference in temperature, the faster the outflow of heat. But, just as the flow of water can be controlled or retarded by dams and channels, the flow of heat can be controlled or retarded by insulation or refrigeration. This is why sea animals are comfortable in water temperatures intolerable to man.

Sea life is equipped by nature to maintain a temperature balance between their bodies and the water. Cold-blooded sea life, such as fish, have no worries in this respect. Their bodies are no warmer than the temperature of the surrounding water. And most of them cannot survive a sudden variation. But warm-blooded mammals such as whales and porpoises must maintain a body heat about the same as that of men. They achieve this by an ingenious combination of insulation and refrigeration that keeps them equally comfortable in the arctic or the tropics.

Heavy layers of blubber covering their bodies is so efficient an insulator that even arctic water does not absorb heat any faster than it is generated inside the whale. In fact, the insulation is so complete that their bodies must be refrigerated to prevent overheating. Their bodies are cooled by pumping blood through their tail flukes, side flukes and dorsal fins. No blubber covers these areas, and thus the blood is cooled by the water. Then, the cooled blood is circulated through the whale's body to keep him at just the right temperature. The refrigeration system through its flukes and fins is automatic and works like a thermostat. Circulation of blood is fast or slow, depending upon the need to maintain the giant body at a constant temperature. As the whale moves south into tropical waters its coat of blubber becomes thinner, and insulation is reduced. But even this efficient refrigeration system could not cool its body fast enough in the heat of tropical air without the reduction of blubber.

Since most of us have little or no blubber to act as insulation, our entire bodies are quickly refrigerated, like the flukes of a giant whale. With chattering teeth and shaking limbs, the shivering divers searched for an answer to the cold. In some cases the cure was worse than the problem. It became a common sight along southern California beaches to see a diver emerge from the water in soaking wet long john underwear sagging around his knees. If these were of any benefit, it was mostly psychological. But perhaps the long johns helped prevent some cuts from sharp rocks and barnacles.

On days when the weather was cold and the water uninviting, the initial shock of contact often discouraged timid divers. Some hardy souls found a certain "cure" for any reluctance to enter the water. Their timidity was overcome and the plunge was actually welcomed when they rubbed their torsos with liniment, which made their skin burn so badly they had to plunge into the water for relief. But they still spent as much time as ever shivering on the beach, and the battle against the cold continued.

Almost every diver had his own pet solution to the problem. A few members of one diving club tried to emulate the Eskimos in their efforts to stay warm. Convinced that the Eskimo diet was responsible for his ability to withstand subfreezing temperatures, the skin divers subsisted on a diet of raw fish and seal blubber for a period of weeks. The experiment was watched with interest by other divers, but the underwater fraternity was spared the ordeal of eating raw fish and blubber when it was learned the diet only made them sick.

Others swore by alcohol as a means to stoke the fire. They

29

claimed it increased circulation and built up body heat. And some of them continued swearing as they were carried in to shore. The reaction from alcohol combined with cold and pressure put them in such a state of shock they were almost paralyzed. Then, shivering and shaking in the heat of a drift-wood fire, new theories were hatched in the fight to beat the cold.

They smeared themselves with hard oil and axle grease. And later, spent hours with kerosene and hot water trying to get it off.

They even tried to boil their long johns in paraffin to make them waterproof. But they only succeeded in burning up the long johns and smoking up their homes.

Nothing seemed to help, and skin divers had given up the battle when news arrived that offered a new hope. World War II was ended and returning servicemen described a rubber suit used by Navy Frogmen. A search was started, a frogman suit was "liberated," a pattern made, and the battle with the cold was won. The first suits were ill-fitting, leaked like a sieve, and it was a terrific struggle to get them on and off. But they worked. For the first time, skin divers were protected from the cold and could stay in the water for hours at any time of the year during any type of weather. American ingenuity and enterprise soon had models in production for distribution across the continent.

The first type of protection was known as a "dry" suit, and wearing one of them was an experience not soon forgotten. They were made of a sheet of thin rubber which covered the skin diver from head to foot. Only the face and hands were exposed to water, and, in extreme cases, the hands were also protected by rubber gloves or mittens. As the name implies, the dry suit keeps a person perfectly dry. Insulation against the cold is obtained by wearing warm clothing underneath the suit. The long johns finally began to do some good, as, when dry, they served the same purpose of maintaining body temperatures as when worn in the air.

Walking into the water with one of these suits on is a peculiar experience. We feel no cold whatsoever. Only the weight of the water pressing against our body gives any indication that we are in the water. As we go deeper, the air in the suit is pushed upwards around our face and we find ourselves encased inside a giant balloon. Unless this air is exhausted, we float high out of the water and are unable to swim or dive. Even when the air is exhausted, the dry underclothing maintains so much buoyancy that a heavy weight belt must be worn to counteract it. With enough weight on our body to give us neutral buoyancy, we can swim in the bulky suit without too much difficulty. Of course, swimming with this equipment on is much slower and more cumbersome than in a bathing suit, but the comfort and extra time in the water make it very much worth while.

With the extensive use of "dry" type suits some new problems were discovered. Our insulation depended upon dry air trapped inside the rubber sheeting of the suit. A tiny pinhole in the rubber caused a leak and, under pressure, let an amazing quantity of water inside the suit. If the leak was small, our bodies warmed the water as it entered and little discomfort was felt at first. But the air inside the suit became moist as water from the leak permeated our underclothing. The moist air impaired our insulation and body heat was conducted away at a rapid rate.

A large rip in a dry suit had an immediate effect. It felt as if a garden hose was suddenly turned on inside the suit. The shock of cold water suddenly flowing over our warm bodies sent many of us scurrying to shore for hasty repairs. A patching kit became an integral part of every diver's pack. A rip in winter water meant the end of insulation and, unless quickly sealed, the diver often spent the balance of the day on shore. But without leaks, the suits gave protection in the coldest water, and divers began to explore virgin areas never before visited by underwater men.

West Coast divers traveled north into the wild and beautiful

31

submarine gardens bordering the coast of Monterey. Here, in 50-degree water, they found volcanic rocks, spectacular caves, and underwater caverns, covered by the most colorful vegetation existing in the sunken world. Strange and varied sea life inhabiting these waters added excitement to the hunt and whetted their curiosity. Encouraged by their success and the protection of cold water suits, they pushed farther northward along the coast. The turbulent waters beneath the raging surf and swirling rip tides of northern California and Oregon were penetrated and explored. Even the cold water of Puget Sound bordering Washington and Canada proved no obstacle with rubber suits, and divers in these quiet, protected waters made their first acquaintance with the giant octopus, dreaded villain of fiction stories, whose ferocious reputation has frightened underwater men since ancient times.

News of the effectiveness of the rubber suits spread across the continent and around the world. In the Great Lakes divers found they could penetrate the thermocline, a layer of ice-cold water which rests beneath the surface of most fresh water lakes. It is a separation of cold water near the bottom and warm water at the surface, as definite as the separation between oil and water. A diver in the thermocline often finds half his body immersed in icy water while the other half is warmed by surface layers. But, with rubber suits, the thermocline was no longer a barrier, and divers began to explore the bottom of lakes. These inland divers discovered wrecks of ancient ships and other relics of the past amazingly well preserved after centuries of submersion. Even wood is unaffected by long periods of immersion in fresh water, corrosion is at a minimum, and the finds were often more than simply treasured souvenirs.

On the east coast of America suit-clad divers worked the frigid waters north of Florida. All of the bays and harbors along the famous New England coast became the playground of skin divers. With no weapons other than their hands, they learned to hunt and capture great clawed lobsters off the coast of Maine. Other hunters armed with spears stalked wary striped bass, tautog and blackfish in a submarine game of hide and seek. But the greatest fascination of the east coast was locating and exploring the hulks of ancient shipwrecks. Since the days of America's first colonists, shallow reefs and rugged headlands bordering harbors and bays along the coast have taken a toll of shipping, and the ocean floor is littered with their hulks. Even the *Andrea Dorea,* which went to the bottom several miles off Nantucket Island in 1956, lies within the range of skin divers, in only 180 feet of water. Unlike the Pacific Coast, which usually drops off sharply into deep water, the Atlantic Coast slopes gradually away from shore, and offers miles of submerged bottom for exploration by skin divers.

Our breakthrough in the battle against the cold water barrier permitted skin diving in such unheard-of places as Norway, Sweden, Iceland, Siberia, and Alaska, and finally, even the unknown waters beneath the frozen wasteland of the arctic were safely penetrated. But before this was accomplished, pioneers experimented with the protection of rubber suits by diving beneath the ice of winter lakes. At first ice diving was done only for adventure and to satisfy curiosity about a frozen world. But the lessons learned from these first experiments paved the way to serious exploration in the arctic. A member of the Chicago Submarine Explorers, Dick Guerine, tells us how it felt to be the first to dive beneath the ice.

"Racine Quarry was frozen solid when we decided on the dive. The idea wasn't new. We had talked about diving in winter for some time, because our summer season was so short. If ice diving proved practical, we could dive all year, and get into places that were too rough or dirty in summer. The lakes have an algae growth when the water is warm that cuts down visibility. In cold water, the algae don't grow and the water is usually crystal clear. With the surface frozen solid, wind couldn't stir up the water, and we would be able to walk right out to our diving spot. Racine Quarry was picked for the first dive because we had been there before and knew the bottom. What we didn't know was how warm we would be wearing rubber suits in ice water, but we intended to find out.

"The whole club went to the quarry, but only two of us made the dive. It was a cloudy day, and the air temperature was 15 degrees, so my partner Bob Dumkowski and I got dressed inside a heated auto, while others chopped a hole through the ice. The ice was 10 inches thick, but the water underneath registered 34 degrees. The only trouble was that everything we got wet froze solid as soon as it hit the air. I wondered if the regulator on my "lung" would still work after it was frozen.

"For the dive, I put on two sets of wool long johns, two pair of socks and some ear muffs like the skiers use to keep their ears warm. My rubber suit had feet and hood built-in, but my hands were ordinarily exposed as the suit was designed to seal at the wrist. To protect my hands, I put a tin can with the ends cut out over my wrists, under the sleeve of the rubber suit. Then I put on wool gloves, and rubber gloves over them. The gauntlet of the rubber gloves was sealed against the sleeve of the suit by wrapping several wraps against the can with a strong elastic band. With my hands protected, the only part of my body in contact with the water would be my face around the mask. My partner was wearing almost the same combination when we donned our masks, flippers, weight belts, and 'lungs' and dropped into the water.

"Since we didn't know what might happen, we had agreed to use a safety line on this first dive. A tender held it at the surface, and I held the other end in my hand. The idea was that if we got into trouble I was to give three hard jerks on the line and the gang would pull us up. We didn't have to give the signal for help, but I was sure glad we had the line before the dive was over.

"We were standing neck deep in ice water, but I didn't feel the cold at all. The gang on shore was actually colder than we were. The 15-degree air seeped through their clothing, and they were shivering and shaking while we were as warm as if we were at home by a fireplace. We let the air out of our suits and went under into one of the strangest and most silent worlds I have ever seen.

"Beneath the surface of the ice the water was absolutely motionless. Even the surface ripples were gone, and the bubbles of exhaled air floated up through the water and then flattened out against the ice like quicksilver. I watched them, fascinated, as they formed fluid, moving patterns that weaved and jiggled as we moved. I was so intent upon other sensations that I didn't even notice the ice water against my face. As we descended, the eerie feeling of quiet was increased by the strangeness of the light. Visibility was surprisingly good, but the light diffused by the ice seemed to glow. No streaks of bright sunlight cut the water. Only a strange, subdued illumination coming from every direction. Except for the noise of our breathing, it was as quiet as a tomb.

"We carried a thermometer to record deep water temperatures. It recorded a steady 34 degrees as deep as 80 feet.

"The only life we saw were tiny mosquito fish, and even these were sluggish in their movements. But we did find the skeleton of an old fishing skiff, with most of its shell intact. We were examining the inside of the skiff when my tank ran out of air. It seemed like only a few moments since we had first entered the water and, at first, I thought that something had gone wrong. But a glance at my watch convinced me that my air was actually gone. We had been underwater half an hour. I signaled Dumkowski that I was out of air, then pulled on my reserve and started back to the surface. Dumkowski and the guide line trailed along behind. And then I made the mistake that taught us a lesson vital to diving through the ice.

"We made no attempt to take up slack in the line leading to the hole at the surface. It never entered our heads that such a guide was necessary. Always before, when a dive was ended, we just swam up until our heads broke through the surface. This time we found the surface covered with an impenetrable lid of ice. Our bubbles of exhaled air flattened out beneath it in grotesque patterns. Bob was also on his reserve, and we would soon be out of air.

"The guide line trailed beneath me to the bottom and, for the first time, I realized that it was impossible to tell in which direction to swim. The hole through the ice was out of sight and the surface under the ice looked exactly the same in all directions. Frantically, I began pulling up the slack and praying that the line was still securely fastened at the hole. The line became taut. But it led at an angle toward the bottom. In silent desperation we pulled ourselves along the line as rapidly as possible. Near the bottom we saw the line caught in an obstruction. Trying to untangle the line almost caused our finish. Our fingers were so numb with cold we couldn't make them work, and my reserve ran out while we were still at it. I was trapped under the ice without air. Momentary panic seized me and I had to fight an urge to streak straight up for the surface. Then, beyond the tangled portion, I saw the line leading along the bottom. On the other end was the hole and safety. I released my grasp on the tangled section and signaled Dumkowski. Holding our breath, we swam as fast as we could toward the entrance at the surface.

"I was gasping for air and on the brink of inhaling water when, like magic, the ice hole appeared before my eyes. It was invisible from a few feet away and would have been impossible to find without the line. My head broke through the surface and I gulped in great quantities of the sweetest air I had ever tasted."

This experience and others similar to it firmly established the necessity of a life line when ice diving even for a short distance in shallow water. Also, unless absolutely necessary, divers underneath a lid of ice never stay until they are down to air reserve. They time their dives and start for the surface while plenty of air remains in their tanks. If a diver does lose

36

sight of the life line and is lost, a rule was established that he go to the surface and remain there until he is found. Search parties can work in circles at the surface much more rapidly than they can search at all depths. If a lost diver remains in one spot he is found very quickly. But if he swims around trying to find the opening, he is apt to drift farther and farther away and may never be located.

There were other hazards from wearing dry suits in addition to the constant threat of rips and tears or getting lost beneath the ice. Our old enemy, the squeeze, returned to plague us once again. As we descended into deep water air inside the suit was compressed, and the suit collapsed against our bodies. In shallow water, less than fifty feet, the squeeze caused only discomfort and a loss of insulation. But in deeper water real trouble was experienced. In some cases the squeeze was so severe that wrinkles in the suit and underclothing actually bruised our skin and we returned to the surface with our bodies covered by angry red welts. One midwest diver was wearing beer can wrist seals during a deep dive in a lake, and at 150 feet the squeeze was so severe the beer cans collapsed against his wrists and he was forced to return quickly to the surface.

We soon learned to pressurize the suits by forcing air into the hoods. Our masks were worn with the rubber edge beneath the seal of the hood. Then, when we blew through our nose, escaping air around the mask entered and filled the suit. It took a little practice before we learned to maintain a balance with the water. If we blew in too much air, the buoyancy caused us to float toward the surface, and the excess air had to be exhausted again before we could submerge. But even pressurizing could get us into trouble unless we were alert. As we ascended from deep water, the inside air expanded, our suits ballooned and accelerated our ascent with an ever increasing speed. The more shallow the water became, the more the air expanded and the faster we shot toward the surface. Unless this ballooning was quickly checked by exhausting the air out of the suits, the rise to the surface was rapid enough to be dangerous.

Ear squeeze also came back with the introduction of dry type suits. The hood of the suits covered our ears and effectively sealed out water pressure. Unlike ear plugs, the suit could not be shot into our ears and rupture eardrums in that manner. But the suits did manage to cause some ruptured eardrums. They ruptured from the inside out. Air pressure, built up inside our middle ear, was so much greater than the slight pressure exerted against the outside of the eardrum that it was pushed outward until it ruptured. Of course, this only occurred in deep water, and only if the suit was not pressurized. But it happened often enough to be a constant worry.

Weight belts worn with cold water suits introduced a new problem. With heavy woolen underclothing beneath the suit, it was often necessary to wear as much as 18 or 20 pounds of lead before we could swim to the bottom. The weights projected from our bodies and were continually catching in weeds and rocks. Sometimes we swam for several seconds without going anywhere before we discovered a weight tangled in kelp and holding us in one place. In an attempt to overcome this problem, one diver at Laguna Beach wore his weights underneath his suit. The experiment caused his death. His weight belt came loose in heavy surf, and the weights dropped down around his ankles, immobilizing his legs. He cried out for help. But before his companions reached him, he disappeared from sight. In the boil and surge of heavy surf it took too long to find him and he was drowned before they got him to the beach.

We learned too that it sometimes became necessary to jettison the weight belt in a hurry. If a dry suit became flooded with water, all buoyancy was lost and we were swimming with the weights dragging us down just as if we were wearing them with bathing suits. For a short distance this could be easily accomplished. But if a diver were exhausted or injured the extra weight was too much for him. After a number of drownings were definitely traced to weight belts, skin divers recommended that the belt be attached only by means of a quick release buckle, which could be operated with one hand. Experience and practice taught us that operating a complicated buckle or knot with both hands was not possible if a diver were already exhausted or injured. He would invariably wait until the last moment before trying to drop his belt. And, by that time, he needed at least one hand free to keep himself afloat.

Many of the complications and problems encountered with dry type suits were overcome with the introduction of "wet" type cold water suits. These derive their name from the fact that water is allowed to seep inside the suit and get the diver wet. Wet suits also give insulation to a swimmer by means of dry air between his body and the water. But with wet suits, the air is trapped in tiny air bubbles inside the material itself instead of being sealed against the diver like in a balloon. The material is a form of sponge rubber which is extremely soft and pliable. But, unlike ordinary sponge, wet suit material is closed cell. Each bubble of air is an individual cell separated from all the rest. For this reason, the material does not absorb water, and air inside the cells always stays dry.

Warmth is obtained from a wet suit only when the suit is fitted to the exact shape of the individual's body. The material must rest snugly against the bare skin of the diver's entire body to form a blanket of dry air separating him from the water. If a wet suit fits loosely, or if any openings occur which allow an interchange of water, insulation is lost and the diver gets cold. But, when the suit is properly fitted, it gives adequate protection in the coldest water. I have worn one a number of times in ice water with very little discomfort from cold.

The wet suit ended our worries about a squeeze. Compression of the air took place within the material with no effect upon the diver. The material was squeezed and became thinner as depth increased and this reduced insulation value, but no diver squeeze occurred. Also, ear squeeze disappeared even when a hood was worn. Since it is not imperative to maintain an airtight seal as with a dry suit, holes could be punched in the wet suit hood over our ears and permit water to enter against our ear drums.

Most of the trouble with leaks went away with the dry suits, too. A leak in a wet suit affects only the area directly beneath the leak and does not destroy the entire insulation, as with a dry suit. Of course, a major rip or tear in a wet suit allows an interchange of water as well as exposing a portion of our body to the cold. If the temperature of the water is very cold, we soon become chilled. The material of wet suits is very fragile and easily ripped, but it is also easily repaired. Even so, the skin-tight fit of these suits makes it necessary that they be put on and taken off with extreme care.

The form-fitting wet suits give us a great deal more freedom in the water than dry suits. There is very little drag, and we can swim with almost the same freedom as in a bathing suit. In fact, the introduction of these suits has spread the popularity of all types of water sports throughout cold water regions. The built-in buoyancy of the material makes them a perfect life preserver as, without weights, a swimmer will float shoulder high out of the water. A person who is unable to swim at all can float around on the surface in perfect safety while wearing one of these suits. He can't sink, the suit keeps him warm, and he soon loses his fear of the water. Wet suits are being adopted for water skiing, surfing, swimming, and all types of water sports wherever the water is too cold for comfort. But their greatest contribution is in Arctic exploration, where exposure to icy water even for short periods can mean death.

Although some Arctic exploration was attempted with only the protection of dry type suits, the danger of a major leak was too great for divers to venture far from shore or the safety of a boat. In rough water, with icy winds and freezing temperatures, the cold from even a small leak could paralyze a diver if he had to swim very far. Also, normal body moisture accumulating inside a dry suit soon created moist air which conducted body heat out into the water at a terrific rate. A perfect answer to conditions of long exposure to freezing water temperatures was found in a combination of wet and dry suit. A wet suit, worn as underclothing beneath a dry suit, gave perfect insulation against the cold. Body moisture was contained inside the wet suit so air trapped by the dry suit remained perfectly dry. Even a rip was sustained in the dry suit, and the diver was sufficiently protected to make a long swim to shore.

A good illustration of the vast field of knowledge opened by this protection is found in the work being done by Bob Jones, a member of the Federal Fish and Wildlife Service, stationed in Cold Bay, Alaska. The temperature of Cold Bay drops to an icy 28 degrees in winter, the coldest water in the world. As a representative of the Fish and Wildlife Service, it is Bob's job to ply the stormy waters of the Aleutian Island chain, checking on all manner of fish and game, both in and out of the water. But his major concern is the pods of sea otters still surviving in the wild, isolated Aleutian waters. These tame sea animals have the most valuable fur in the world, and at one time were hunted so extensively that they were thought to have been exterminated. Sale of sea-otter fur has been banned for fifty years, but just before they were taken off the market, one fur alone sold for over $20,000. Today, under protection of dedicated men such as Bob Jones, the sea otter population is coming back, and the pods are closely guarded against illegal depredation.

But Bob wasn't satisfied with casual observation of the otters from the surface. He was curious about their food supply, the lowly sea urchin, and wondered about many questions that could only be answered through underwater ob-

41

servation. Although he always works alone, in violation of a basic safety rule of diving, he had no choice. The closest diving buddy to Cold Bay, Alaska was in Anchorage, a thousand miles away. But safety is a lifelong habit with a man of Bob's profession. His work takes him to isolated regions in subzero weather, where he spends months relying on himself and the equipment he carries. This training and background had taught him to be careful, and skin diving by himself was just one more accomplishment in a life filled with adventure.

At first, with only a dry suit for protection, his explorations were limited to short periods, close to shore. No warming house awaited him if his suit developed a leak, and in 28-degree water, exposure for a few minutes could bring paralysis and death. But these short dives in shallow water only whetted his appetite for more. To continue his exciting studies of virgin underwater territory, it was imperative that a better and safer protection from cold water be found. With this in mind, Bob contacted one of America's leading manufacturers of cold water diving suits and presented his ideas, obtained from long experience in cold weather. Together, Bob and the manufacturer worked out a Vapor Barrier suit which proved to be the answer to his problem. At the time, wet suits were in their infancy, and as yet, unsatisfactory in ice water. The Vapor Barrier was a thin wet suit, worn next to Bob's body, then two sets of long underwear, followed by a dry suit. Mittens instead of gloves covered his hands for greater warmth. With this equipment Bob could stay in 28-degree water for five hours without getting cold, and he was in the suit a total of nine hours during subzero weather. His safety was also greatly increased. On one dive, the dry suit sustained a rip over a foot long and it took Bob fifteen minutes to reach shore. Such a rip, and the subsequent exposure would probably have proved fatal earlier. But this time he felt only a slight discomfort, and could have remained in the water a great deal longer without danger. As Bob states it himself, "When our cold water equipment reached a satisfactory point, results began to accrue.

"Our first success with the cold water diving gear was in capturing sea otter. We do this on the beaches and off-shore rocks of Amchitka most successfully during heavy storms. The biggest problem was to reach the off-shore rocks under these conditions without wrecking the dory and ourselves when attempting a landing. With the cold water suit, I swam to the rocks and caught the otters when conditions were too rough to make a landing with the dory.

"Perhaps the most useful thing we can do with diving gear is to learn the conditions under which the sea otter gets its food, and to learn the extent of food available to them. We are conducting such a study at Adak, in the western Aleutians, where a rapidly growing population of sea otters exists. Such studies are commonly used in management of range and browse animals. Random plots are marked, and the vegetative cover is analyzed and recorded to show what suitable forage exists, and to serve as a comparison with other areas, and to establish a standard which can be continuously observed as the animals utilize it. We are now doing the same sort of thing with sea otters, utilizing the diving gear for obtaining the information. As an example of what the sea can produce, one sample taken from a square yard yielded $32\frac{1}{2}$ pounds of edible invertebrates, chiefly blue mussels."

Bob's studies disclosed such a tremendous amount of information and data about unclassified sea life that the Fish and Wildfile Service is considering stationing a full-time marine biologist at Cold Bay, just for the purpose of classifying and identifying the new discoveries he is making. Bob may also be sent to Scripps Institute of Oceanography for a course in marine biology to help him in this new field. Bob's work is just one example of the many fields of research and discovery which have been opened by development of effective cold water protection.

Breathing Underwater and the Problem of Changing Pressures

THE major difference between breathing equipment used by skin divers and previous types of equipment is our present independence. We have no air hose or connecting lines to the surface, and are completely free to move about, as our air supply is carried in a tank on our back. The term, self-contained underwater breathing apparatus, has been reduced to "scuba," a name coined from the first letters of the definition. This name is used in reference to all makes and types of self-contained units. Scuba diving is causing a revolution in underwater exploration, salvage, science, and treasure hunting as well as in underwater sports. But learning its limitations and possibilities are necessary before the thrills and excitement can be enjoyed.

The lessons learned with mask and flippers cost us some ruptured eardrums, black eyes and a few hard knocks against the rocks, but fatalities were rare. While holding our breath, an instinctive caution prevented us from going beyond our limits. We knew our time was short and we hesitated to enter areas of possible danger until we were sure we could escape. But, with breathing equipment, all of this was changed. It permitted novice divers to go deeper and stay longer than any of us before, and it introduced a whole new series of underwater safety rules. These rules were slowly and painfully learned, and cost the lives of many divers. Skin diving with breathing apparatus can be as safe as ordinary swim-

Instruction and practice with equipment are important. Here author Lloyd Bridges demonstrates to a swimming pool class. (*Paul Tzimoulis*)

Skin diving search and rescue teams are becoming increasingly important to emergency operations in drowning cases. Here a Douglas Aircraft rescue team demonstrates the speed and effectiveness of helicopters used to transport skin divers. Action took place in Pacific off Santa Monica harbor.

The wild and turbulent surf off a rocky coastline presents a formidable obstacle to skin divers entering the water. Note the long underwear worn to protect the dry suit from rips and snags. (*Julius Downs*)

A scuba diver entering the water from a height must hold to his mask in order to prevent its being knocked off his face. Such entries should first be practiced from the edge of a swimming pool. (*Skin Diver Magazine*)

(*Top, left*) In the surge of shallow, turbulent surf, safe practice is to stay low and hang on until the surge subsides. (*Top, right*) Care must be taken to select a point of entry and exit which provides the greatest safety from surf and surge. Author Lloyd Bridges demonstrates entry on the protected side of a point. (*Bottom, left*) A fully equipped diver must have a boarding ladder when working from a boat. Even then it is sometimes necessary to remove flippers and tank before attempting to climb the ladder. Note the clothing of the deck crew bundled against the cold. A skin diver insulated by a wet suit is often warmer underwater than spectators who remain perfectly dry. (*Bottom, right*) As Mike Nelson, Lloyd Bridges lives an exciting life. Here he is called upon to wrestle an alligator.

Larry Beals and Mac Thompson hold two giant octopuses captured in the depths of Puget Sound. Note the jet of water streaming from the sac of the larger octopus as it continues its struggle to escape. (*Bud Abbey*)

Murray Heminger, of the Kona Coast, Hawaii, demonstrates his skill with a Hawaiian sling gun. Note the extra free spears carried in his hand, some with fish impaled on the barbs. Carrying fish on a string or on extra spears is common practice in some diving grounds, but in shark-infested waters this can be dangerous. (*Skin Diver Magazine*)

A great, man-killing shark is a fearful and thrilling sight when viewed beneath the surface. (*Hans Haas*)

Al Tlam and Fred Mase of the Minnesota Skin Divers check an ice-covered location in preparation for a dive. (*Bob Travis Keagle*)

Lloyd Bridges examines an interesting relic taken from the ocean floor by his twelve-year-old son, Jeff. It is such bits of innocent evidence which lead to the discovery of famous wrecks and sometimes sunken treasure.

ming, but when the rules are unknown or ignored, tragedy can strike quickly.

An example of such a tragedy, caused by ignorance, occurred while I was diving off the Long Beach breakwater. A companion and I were snorkeling for fish when another boat dropped anchor, and a young fellow began struggling into a brand new "lung." I watched him until my companion surfaced with a nice bass on the end of his spear and I lost interest in activity aboard the boat. I snorkeled for a moment to catch my breath, then drifted to the bottom in search of a sea food dinner. A wary bass played hide and seek with me through the breakwater, but it finally disappeared deep inside a crevice. On the way back to the surface I passed the diver wearing the tank. He was headed toward the bottom and waved a friendly greeting as we passed.

Later, on the surface, his head shot out of the water, and he yelled one word, "Help," then sank back out of sight. I dived, and found him sinking to the bottom. Blood trickled from his mouth and his eyes were staring, wide. The mouthpiece of his breathing unit was dangling in the water.

I towed him to the surface and put him on the boat, but he died before we could get him to a doctor. An autopsy later verified what I suspected. He had suffered an air embolism from expanding air inside his lungs. His equipment had functioned perfectly but the diver had held his breath when he started for the surface. The result is the opposite of a squeeze.

With breathing equipment we must not only equalize pressures as we descend, we must also equalize internal pressure from expanding air as we ascend. While underwater, the air we breathe is compressed in volume by the pressure of the water. If a balloon is fully inflated underwater it will explode as it rises to the surface, because the air inside expands as it rises. The same thing can happen inside our lungs if we hold our breath. The expansion of air ruptures tiny lung tissues, air is released into our blood stream, and, if the air bubbles lodge in our heart or brain, we die of an embolism. Fortunately, embolism is simple to avoid. If we continue breathing at all times, excess air is exhausted, and a balance maintained. *Never hold your breath as you ascend.* If your tank is out of air, exhale all the way to the surface. Ignorance of this basic precaution has killed more skin divers than all other causes combined. An embolism cannot occur while snorkel diving, as our lungs are inflated on the surface at atmospheric pressure.

One of the major advantages of modern breathing equipment is that it automatically adjusts and balances the pressure of the air we breathe according to the depth of the water in which we are swimming. We have no valves to fiddle with, no surface connections to worry about, and we are as free as the fish around us. Throughout the world enthusiastic skin divers demanded compact breathing equipment long before it was commercially produced. It is interesting that, even though the basic principles of automatic pressure regulation were known and had been applied to underwater breathing as long ago as 1866, self-contained underwater breathing equipment could not be put to practical use until flippers gave us swimming ability almost equal to a fish. Only then could the age-old concept of "walking" on the bottom be discarded. Leaded shoes, heavy weights and cumbersome helmets were no longer necessary, and men began to think of equipment adapted to this new-found freedom. But the environment hasn't changed and some of the problems of rapidly changing pressures, which have plagued divers throughout history, are still with us today. Unless these problems are clearly understood, they can get us into trouble just as easily as they did the ancient divers. But, we can avoid mistakes made in the past by knowing what they were, and learning what caused them.

At first glance, taking an air supply underwater seems a simple matter. Every day, in my mail, I receive at least one question which asks, "How deep can I breathe with a snorkel?"

Or they want to know why the tube of a snorkel is not made longer so a skin diver can breathe while he is on the bottom. The idea of a tube extending from the diver's mouth to the surface has been tried since the time of the ancient Greek sponge divers. I tried it once in a swimming pool, and was amazed at the difficulty in breathing even a few feet beneath the surface. The weight of the water pressing against my chest made it almost impossible to inflate my lungs with my head only two feet below the surface. To discover the reason, I placed a piece of garden hose in the pool and tried blowing air out of the end. To my surprise it was impossible to force out any air at all, with the end of the hose 6 feet below the surface. With the hose 3½ feet deep only a trickle of bubbles appeared.

After this experience my respect for the skin diving ability of the American Indian increased immeasurably. There are authentic accounts of Indians catching ducks by swimming among them while submerged, and breathing through a reed extended above the surface. A skilled skin diver would have difficulty duplicating such a feat without disturbing the water surface, and the ducks.

Naturally, after it was learned that our lungs are not strong enough to lift the tremendous weight of water, the next step was an attempt to force air down through the tube. But this idea ran into a number of complications. First, the water pressure had to be overcome before any air at all went through the tube. And the water pressure varied with each change in depth. Water weighs approximately one half pound for each foot. At 50 feet, 25 pounds of air pressure was required to force a small amount of air out of the end of the tube. When a pump was found to produce the needed pressure, we learned it lacked the necessary volume. Had we been familiar with Boyle's law of compressed gases, we would have understood our trouble. In effect, this law states that the volume of gas inside a container is directly proportional to its pressure. Air at sea level is under 14.7 pounds of atmospheric pressure (1 atmosphere). Gas in a cylinder on the surface under 10 atmospheres of pressure contains twice as much as under 5 atmospheres. Underwater each 33 feet of depth is equivalent to one additional atmosphere of pressure. For this reason our lungs, when completely filled at a depth of 33 feet, hold twice as much air as when filled at the surface. And for each additional 33 feet of depth, the volume

BOYLE'S & CHARLES' LAWS
OF COMPRESSED GASES

SEA LEVEL	ABSOLUTE PRESSURE		
1 Atmosphere	14.7 P.S.I.	1 Cu. ft. Air	4 Cu. ft.
33'- 2 Atmospheres	29.4 P.S.I.	1/2 Cu. ft. Air	2 Cu. ft.
66'- 3 Atmospheres	44.1 P.S.I.	1/3 Cu. ft. Air	1 1/3 Cu. ft
99'- 4 Atmospheres	58.8 P.S.I.	1/4 Cu. ft. Air	1 Cu. ft.

of air required to fill our lungs is increased accordingly. At 66 feet we are under 3 atmospheres of pressure, and our lungs hold three times as much air. At 99 feet they hold four times as much, and so on as deep as we can go. Another way of putting it is that a balloon filled with one cubic foot of air on the surface will be reduced to one half a cubic foot at 33 feet, one third its size at 66 feet, and so on. The chart on this page illustrates Boyle's law, and from it we can see why large volumes of air are required for breathing in deep water.

Even when volume was increased, the problem was not solved. With a continuous flow of air from the end of the tube, a diver couldn't hold it in his mouth. After considerable practice he could stay underwater by breathing from the tube and holding his breath while he worked. But this was extremely inefficient, and little actual work could be accomplished.

Several innovations were tried to make the air hose work. An airtight, flexible bag was inserted in the hose close to the diver's mouth and served as a reservoir from which he could inhale. An escape valve on the bag exhausted excess air and exhalations so the hose could remain always in the diver's mouth. But, once again, pressure differentials defeated the idea. It had the same effect as breathing through a tube in shallow water. The bag floated above the diver's head and was under a lower pressure than his lungs. The effort required to pull air from the bag was about the same as pulling air through a tube in a few feet of water. If the bag was weighted to sink below the diver's waist, the process was reversed. Pressure squeezed air from the bag to the end of the hose, and the diver received a constant flow of air with which he couldn't cope. Also, the buoyant bag was difficult to handle and constantly interfered with the diver's movements.

The bag idea was finally abandoned in favor of a heavy bell suspended on a cable. Air pumped from the surface was trapped beneath the bell, and remained in constant balance with the pressure of the water. Excess air pumped into the bell escaped out of the bottom. Insufficient air let water rise inside the bell until pressures were balanced. But in either case, a diver with his head inside the bell could breathe just as if he were treading water on the surface. At first these were used only as stationary storage chambers from which divers worked while holding their breath. In some cases the chambers were monstrous and could hold a small army of underwater warriors at one time. But the need for mobile breathing methods led to constant improvements. Finally the bell was reduced in size, a window was installed, and the forerunner of modern helmet equipment was developed.

With mobile helmets the diver's feet were weighted so he could remain upright on the bottom. The helmet was also weighted to overcome the buoyancy of air trapped inside. With a window inserted in the helmet wall and a flexible hose supplying air from the surface, the diver could move slowly about over the ocean floor. This ancient method of diving is still popular in some shallow water areas, and is so simple to construct that a number of youngsters have run into trouble by using homemade gear. I had such an experience myself when I was entering my teens.

Three of us got the idea from an abandoned water heater. We spent weeks cutting it in half with a hack saw and installing a plastic window. We hooked an old garden hose to one of the top water pipes and used it for an air hose. Our compressor and pump came from my dad's paint sprayer, which I "borrowed" from the garage. We tied enough chunks of old lead and iron around the bottom of the shell to make sure it would sink, and for weighted shoes we tied some pieces of old railroad track to the bottoms of our feet. Then we played it careful and smart, we thought, by having sense enough to "test" the outfit before we actually tried it. But remembering that test now makes me shudder. It consisted simply of dropping the tank into the lake from the end of a pier and then swimming down and going inside to see if it held air. Of course it did, and some of us actually took a couple of breaths before we swam to the surface. Why we didn't kill ourselves with embolisms is something I will never understand, for we now know from sad experience that this has killed some divers in less than ten feet of water. Had we filled our lungs completely full with air from the sunken helmet, then held our breath as we surfaced, they no doubt would have ruptured on the way up, and this book would never have been written.

After the test, we drew straws to see who would be first, and I was "lucky." The others manned the compressor to try and keep it working while I eagerly tied the weights to my feet, put on the helmet and slipped down into the water.

Everything was wonderful at first, and I found myself enchanted by my new surroundings. Through the window of the helmet I could see the bottom of the lake and my feet kicked up clouds of smoky dust which drifted through the water behind me as I shuffled along. Occasionally a school of tiny fish would dart around my head, chasing each other in their endless underwater games. Once I was thrilled by the sight of a big perch which nosed up against the glass until it saw my eyes or something which frightened it away. Each time I inhaled, water would rise slightly inside the helmet, but was pushed down again when I exhaled. Once I bent too far and tipped the helmet on its side so that the air spilled out and the water was up to my nose before I righted it. But the compressor soon pushed the water down again, and I continued on my way.

Then suddenly I noticed that the water was rising. It was already high on my chest, and creeping toward my neck. I could breathe as long as my mouth and nose were in an air pocket, but, no matter how hard I exhaled, the water continued slowly climbing and I was sure it would soon fill the entire inside of the helmet. Cautiously I reached down and tried to untie the weights on my feet. But I couldn't see, and my hands fumbled with the knots. If I looked down, my head was in the water and I couldn't breathe. I started walking back in the direction of the pier, hoping my companions would see my trouble before it was too late. But the water continued rising and reached my chin. If I stumbled or breathed deeply, my mouth and nose went under until I exhaled and blew it down again. Frightened and desperate, I held my breath while I ducked my head and tried again to untie the weights on my feet. This time I managed to free one foot. But when I went up inside the helmet for air, only my nose came above the water. Even after I exhaled, so little air remained that I couldn't get a full breath. I was beginning to panic, and was frantically trying to free my other foot when two powerful hands caught me by the shoulders and raised me to the surface.

My dad had missed his compressor and traced us to the pier. He found two worried boys trying to start the compressor, and learned that I was still underwater. Without hesitation, he had plunged in and found me struggling with the weights. I will never know if I could have broken free without his help, but his orders to abandon the experiment were unnecessary. That old, makeshift helmet is probably still lying on the bottom of the lake. None of us ever went back down to get it.

In 1837, a London engineer named Augustus Siebe developed a small helmet attached to a full length suit, and a revolution in underwater diving began. Modifications of his suit are conventional diving dress today. The helmet, or hard-hat divers, regulated the flow of air into their suits by means of valves operated by hand. Exhaust valves are installed to bleed away excess air and maintain a balance inside the suit according to the depth in which the diver is working. The suit, designed to enable a diver to walk on the bottom, is heavily weighted so he can stay in one spot and do heavy work. But his mobility is limited; when his depth is changed, the valves must be adjusted accordingly, or the suit will receive air faster than it can be exhausted, and so the diver could "blow up," a term used to describe what happens when a helmet suit becomes too buoyant, and begins to float to the surface. As the diver rises, air in his suit expands, and he shoots to the surface with arms and legs extended by the inflated suit, rendering him helpless. Or, if he suddenly drops into deeper water without increasing his air intake, he is subject to a squeeze. A severe squeeze in one of these suits can mash a diver's body into the rigid helmet to balance the tremendous increase of water pressure.

But modern deep sea suits have built-in check valves and automatic adjustments to provide greater safety and more efficient operation. For heavy work and long periods of submersion, the helmet diver is by far the most efficient. But in shallow water, or for light salvage and survey work, the skin diver has the advantage. So much so that most deep sea salvage companies, which at first considered scuba equipment nothing but a toy, are now employing it extensively in commercial operations.

The idea of self-contained diving is not new. Compressed air and oxygen were used a number of times to permit breathing independent of surface connections. But, in each case, the compressed air supply was provided in connection with conventional, "walk around" equipment, and met with little success. The popularity of skin diving with mask, flippers, and snorkel created a demand for light weight, self-contained breathing equipment adapted to the sport, and the result was inevitable. Practically all of the old, discarded ideas reappeared as well as some new ones, which are still in use today.

The first self-contained diving unit was invented by W. H. James, as long ago as 1825. It was intended for use with conventional diving dress, and supplied oxygen inside the suit from a cylinder. It had two major obstacles which limited its use. The first was that CO_2 (carbon dioxide) exhaled was not absorbed, but was allowed to build up with the breathing mixture. As a result, either the diver's time was extremely limited, or he ran into dangerous concentrations of CO_2. Also, at that time, high pressure cylinders were not produced commercially, and the maximum pressure in the containers was 30 atmospheres. This compares to cylinders in present-day apparatus with pressures of over 200 atmospheres.

In 1878, the first really practical self-contained breathing unit was developed by H. A. Fleuss, of Siebe Gorman and Company, of England. It was a closed circuit, oxygen regenerating unit with an absorbent to remove exhaled CO_2 and moisture. Oxygen, supplied by cylinders carried on the diver's back or chest, was admitted into a breathing bag by manually controlled valves. Exhaled air passed into another bag containing an absorbent for CO_2, and then was recirculated into the inhalation bag to be rebreathed. This was later improved so that oxygen was admitted automatically through a reducing valve, and no manual manipulation by the diver was required. These units were used extensively for a number of years in shallow water operations and in atmospheres of poisonous gases. But they were designed and used with helmets and weighted feet for walking on the bottom, which limited their use.

Oxygen rebreathers came into widespread use during World War II, when the U.D.T. or Navy Frogmen used them in underwater warfare. With only a small cylinder of oxygen as an air supply, these units could be used for two hours of submersion without requiring a return to the surface. Their light weight, combined with extended diving time was considered ideal, as divers could work underwater, close to shore without being observed. But their depth was restricted to 33 feet. Below this depth, the diver breathed pure oxygen under two atmospheres of pressure, and was in danger of oxygen poisoning. For many years it wasn't known exactly what caused this poisoning. But a number of accidents disclosed that a diver breathing pure oxygen in deep water could pass out without previous warning symptoms. The fact that it didn't happen every time gave rise to considerable controversy and confusion, and this led to many unnecessary deaths.

After the war, oxygen rebreathers were released to surplus stores for sale to the general public. Commercial manufacturing firms also produced them in quantities, and many prominent divers extolled their virtues. A number of these divers went so far as to claim the rebreathers were not at all dangerous in shallow water, and were safe in deep water if used only for short periods. The cheapness of surplus rebreathers, and the length of time they lasted underwater, made them extremely attractive, until the danger was fully understood and skin diving clubs and *The Skin Diver* magazine spread a warning against them throughout the world. During the

54

period of their popularity, such divers as Hans Haas used them extensively and extolled them in published books. The extreme danger of using oxygen under water is illustrated by the experience of a friend of mine, Bill Smithson, who almost died while using one. He tells it in his own words and, fortunately for me, his experience occurred early in my diving career, or I might have joined the ranks of skin divers killed by oxygen poisoning.

"I won't mention the name of the firm that hired me to demonstrate the unit, because they are still in business and, at the time, we both thought oxygen rebreathers were perfectly safe if used in shallow water. I had been demonstrating the unit for two years, over the United States. It had never given me a bit of trouble and, until the day of the accident, I would have staked my life on its safety. In fact, that is exactly what I did.

"One day I was demonstrating in a swimming pool in front of a large audience. Everything was going fine. The unit was working perfectly, as I put it through the usual routine. Then I decided to demonstrate how fast a swimmer could move with it, and put on a burst of speed. I was breathing faster than normal, but getting plenty of air, when I suddenly blacked out. There was absolutely no warning. One minute I was swimming in the pool, and the next thing I knew, I awakened in a hospital.

"My friends told me later that I had been motionless for quite a while before they decided something was wrong and pulled me out. That's another feature of a closed circuit unit, which sometimes can be a disadvantage. No bubbles show to tell anyone if you are breathing or not. They had to give me artificial respiration, call an inhalator squad, and even then it was nip and tuck for quite a while. That's as close as I ever came to cashing in my chips and it sure convinced me that oxygen rebreathers are not safe, even in shallow water."

Hans Haas, in his book *Men and Sharks,* describes a similar experience which he attributes to cold water. He claims a diver can become so cold he will pass out without warning. I have been so cold my vision blurred and I lost all sense of direction, but I have never passed out from this cause. However, a diver breathes more rapidly when he is cold, and consequently consumes more oxygen. Possibly this accounts for an oxygen blackout in shallow water.

But, in spite of these dangers, divers continued using oxygen in closed circuit units. Sometimes skin divers throughout an entire area are influenced in their selection of equipment by the opinions and preferences of one or two key personalities in a diving club. This is wonderful, as long as the knowledge of the leaders is based on fact. But, as in the case of rebreathers, if the leadership is wrong, the lives of hundreds of divers may be endangered.

For years some of my skin diving friends in Canada and New Zealand insisted upon using oxygen in spite of warnings of its danger. They were thoroughly convinced that our fears were groundless, and that the accidents we mentioned were due to faulty equipment or lack of knowledge. Their letters proudly announced that, among the hundreds of club members using oxygen, not one fatality had occurred. Both of these friends were skin diving pioneers and highly respected for their knowledge of the sport. They loved rebreathers because they were easily available in their country, were cheap to buy and cheap to use, and lasted longer underwater. This opinion cost both of them their lives. The Canadian died while giving a demonstration in shallow water off the end of a public pier. He surfaced and yelled "hey," then sank beneath the water. An autopsy disclosed that he had died of a massive embolism, but he was too experienced a diver to get an embolism from holding his breath. His death was traced directly to the rebreather. The New Zealand diver was discovered unconscious on the bottom, and we can only guess as to the cause. But after the death of these leaders the clubs abandoned rebreathers for safer methods.

It has been determined that the cause of oxygen poisoning is the increased absorption of the gas under pressure. At 33 feet, or two atmospheres, the gas is under twice the pressure and is more readily absorbed by our blood stream. The hemoglobin in our blood has such an affinity for oxygen that it becomes completely saturated. With no corpuscles available to carry away carbon dioxide with exhaled air, the trouble is actually CO_2 poisoning. This poisoning can also occur in shallow water, if the diver is working hard, and his rate of breathing is increased. Becoming cold also causes rapid breathing, with the same effect.

An open circuit breathing apparatus is one in which the exhaled air is not rebreathed but discarded into the water. For many years this type was unsatisfactory for self-contained diving because of the extremely short duration of a dive. A constant flow of air to a face mask or breathing bag soon exhausted the supply. The answer to this problem of wasted air was a demand regulator, which adjusts itself automatically to the pressure of surrounding water, and gives air only as the diver inhales. The first of these, designed for underwater use, was invented by Benoist Rouquarol, almost a hundred years ago, and his design is so similar to the modern scuba we wonder that it was never accepted. The patent, with a detailed description of his demand regulator for underwater use, has been available as U.S. Patent #59,529 since 1866. The drawings and descriptions contained in his early patent papers give us an understanding of the working of modern scuba. Also, it indicates the reason his device was not adopted at the time. In clear, concise wording he describes the operation of his unit.

"Be it known that I, Benoist Rouquarol, of Paris, in the Empire of France, have invented certain new and improved Apparatus for Regulating the Flow of Gases; and I hereby declare the following to be a full, clear, and exact description of the same. . . .

"The apparatus I have invented is intended to regulate the

flow of compressed gasses, and to furnish the diver or workman who employs it respirable air under a pressure equal to that of the medium in which he is.

"The construction and arrangement of this apparatus are very simple, as will be seen by reference to the drawings.

". . . A reservoir of any suitable form—as, for instance, cylindrical containing air compressed to a degree which may be equivalent of 40 atmospheres. (Cylinders withstanding greater pressures were not in production. Today's cylinders withstand over 200 atmospheres.)

"Above the reservoir is formed the air chamber which communicates to said reservoir through an orifice provided with a valve which is operated by a stem or rod secured—to the cover of the chamber. This cover, made of gutta-percha (rubber) or other suitable flexible and elastic material, strengthened or braced at its center by a wooden or metal disc, is secured around the upper part of the chamber by a metal belt or band. A gutta-percha tube extends from this chamber to the mouth of the diver, who carries on his back the apparatus just described.

"From this arrangement of parts it results that if the exterior pressure exceeds that of the air inclosed in the chamber, the elastic cover will be depressed, carrying with it the movement of the rod, which, by opening the check valve, will allow a certain quantity of air from the reservoir to pass into the chamber. The workman will thus be constantly supplied with air, which comes to him under a pressure equivalent to that of the medium in which he is."

Rouquarol goes on to describe the nonreturn exhaust valve attached to the chamber which permits air exhaled into the chamber to escape. What he described is the basic principle of modern demand regulators which make self-contained diving as simple as swimming. With improvements and modifications, underwater breathing was made perfectly safe for the average swimmer with only moderate training in its use. Probably Rouquarol's scuba didn't catch the popular fancy because of handicaps in securing material. Also, flippers were unknown, and no skin divers were around to serve as eager customers. His 40 atmospheres of pressure would have given a very short immersion time, and his reference to rubber as "gutta-percha" is an indication of the quality of rubber products available in his day.

A demand regulator, such as Rouquarol described, gives air at the same pressure as the depth of water. The key to its operation is the flexible diaphragm exposed to water pressure on one side and air pressure on the other. Movement of the diaphragm releases air from the cylinder. The diaphragm is adjusted so that when air pressure and water pressure are equal the air is shut off. When a diver inhales through a hose opening, air pressure is reduced, the diaphragm is pushed down by the water, and opens a valve admitting a flow of air from the cylinder. When inhalation stops, air pressure builds up underneath until it equals the water pressure, and the flow of air is shut off. Air and water pressure are always in balance no matter at what depth the diver is working. The beauty of this arrangement is its simplicity and its automatic operation. The diver only needs to continue breathing and the regulator does all of the adjusting.

On March 10, 1947, Jacques Yves Cousteau and Emile Gagnan of Paris, France, obtained a United States Patent for an improved type of demand regulator for underwater breathing. Their scuba was made available to skin divers under the trade name "Aqua Lung." In this unit the regulator was separate from the compressed air tanks, and two hoses led to the mouthpiece instead of the single hose devised by Rouquarol. One hose served for inhalation and one for exhalation, so the diver would not at any time rebreathe his exhaled air. The exhaust of the exhalation hose was stationed close to and directly over the diaphragm to insure that air would come to the diver easily while his body was in any position in the water. Without this arrangement, in some positions breathing would be difficult, and in others air would flow continuously. These principles are now incorporated in all modern scuba, and underwater breathing is almost as natural as breathing on the surface.

Skin divers may now select breathing apparatus from a wide assortment and from a number of manufacturers. All incorporate demand regulators in one form or another, designed to provide an ample supply of air at any reasonable depth. The primary difference in design is aimed either at greater safety and dependability in the unit, or at a more simple system offered at a lower cost. Preference among divers for the different types of scuba is as varied, and as prejudiced, as preference among automobile owners for different makes of cars. And the differences are in much the same category. Almost any modern scuba in good condition will give satisfactory performance. But, as with most other products, the customer usually gets quality in proportion to the price.

A two-stage regulator is the most expensive, and is usually more dependable. In this, high pressure air from the cylinder is reduced to a lower pressure before contact with the diaphragm. The purpose is to provide a constant pressure against the mechanism of the demand valve regardless of varying pressures in the cylinder. Ease of breathing is adjusted for this constant pressure and little variation is encountered. Single-stage units eliminate the high pressure reduction valve and consequently can be produced at a lower cost. In these, high cylinder pressures are reduced for breathing by action of the sensitive demand regulator. They require a fine adjustment and careful maintenance to balance breathing action against varying pressure as the cylinder empties. But, as stated before, in good condition and properly maintained, a single-stage regulator gives dependable performance.

A recent addition to the scuba family are single hose units. These are two stage, but the high pressure reduction takes place in a valve at the cylinder. From this valve air is conducted through a special hose to a demand regulator attached directly to the mouthpiece. In this type the air hose cannot fill with water as long as pressure remains in the cylinder. Need for an exhalation hose is eliminated by attaching the regulator and exhaust valve directly to the mouthpiece.

Skin divers now have a choice of small cylinders, large cylinders or single, double and triple tank blocks to give any quantity of air supply desired. Also available are small, portable air compressors especially designed for filling scuba tanks, which can be transported to isolated regions, and provide an unlimited supply of diving air. But none of the scubas are designed for pure oxygen, and using this gas in place of atmospheric air is very dangerous. Only pure, carefully filtered air should be used at any time in diving.

The development of scuba, with its low cost, automatic operation, and simplicity, introduced laymen to the adventure and excitement of the world beneath the surface, and began an underwater revolution.

5

Scuba Limitations—How Safety Rules Were Learned

THE introduction of scuba excited the imagination of skin divers throughout the world, and its simplicity attracted millions of new adherents. For the first time in history the mysteries of deep water could be explored by an average person at little cost, and with practically no training. Diving was almost as simple as swimming. The automatic operation of demand regulators adjusted pressure to any depth. Our bodies were inflated by air pressure and sustained the weight of water in the same manner as air compressed into an automobile tire withstands the weight of the car. Simply by donning a face mask, flippers, and a tank of air, a whole new world was opened. The scuba took us into deep mysterious canyons and crevices where we made the aquaintance of strange sea life, weird vegetation, and the wrecks of sunken ships. It took us deep beneath the surface of clear water lakes and rivers in search of relics from the past which had lain undisturbed for centuries. But breathing air underwater introduced novices to hazards with which even veteran snorkel divers were unfamiliar. An entirely new set of safety rules had to be learned through bitter experience.

Until scuba was introduced, skin divers were primarily sportsmen, and the technical language of commercial divers was foreign to us. We had no instruction books or pamphlets warning of the danger of embolism, bends, squeeze, Boyle's law, Dalton's law, or Henry's law. Instead, salesmen and promoters, anxious to realize profits from the sale of scuba, extolled the virtues and simplicity of its use with complete disregard for any need of safety measures. It was acclaimed as a new toy for underwater swimming which anyone could use without instruction. In fact, many claimed it was so "foolproof" that it could be safely used by people unable to swim. That so many of us could survive this period of ignorance was due to the work of dedicated members in skin diving clubs and their magazine, *The Skin Diver*. As soon as dangers were discovered and safety lessons learned, these people sounded a warning which spread across the continent and throughout the world. But, unfortunately, the glamour of underwater adventure overshadowed the need for safety and too many untrained divers lost their lives before the rules were learned.

We had to learn not only the poisonous effect of air under pressure and how deep was "too deep" with this new toy. We had to learn, through sad experience, simple precautions which were unknown at the time. One of these involved the weight of an empty scuba tank, and learning it almost cost the life of Bill Barada. From his story we can appreciate the value of training and experience. Let's listen while he tells us what happened when he used one of the first scubas imported to America.

"I think it was 1949 when Rene Bussoz sold me my first lung. He had imported them from France with an exclusive license to manufacture the Aqua Lung over here. I bought one of the first twenty he sold out of his store in Westwood, California, before it became U.S. Divers Company, and I still remember his instructions when I asked him how to use it. He said, 'There is nothing to it. Just put it on and breathe. The lung does all the work, it's foolproof.' With this assurance, I put the tank aboard my boat and headed for Emerald Bay at Catalina Island.

"I was all alone aboard the boat. The buddy system was

unknown and it wasn't unusual for divers to work by themselves. I put on a dry type suit, 18 pounds of weight, mask, flippers, then strapped the lung on good and tight so it couldn't come loose. At first my mask leaked a little, and I had to keep bobbing back to the surface to dump the water out. But, I finally got it to seal, and had a chance to look around. It was a strange feeling to be able to breathe underwater and stay down as long as I wanted. The air came easily each time I inhaled, and I left a string of bubbles streaking toward the surface when I exhaled. After a few minutes my confidence increased, and I dropped into deep water for a look at bottom I had never seen. The tank on my back was buoyant so I felt no weight, and I could move through the water with surprising ease. It was a new experience to take my time looking into crevices and caves, and I forgot to watch the time. It seemed I had been under only a few minutes when it suddenly became extremely hard to breathe.

"I was sure something had gone wrong. Rene had told me the 38-cubic-foot tank would give half an hour of diving. I still wasn't in any trouble. The depth was only sixty feet, and, from snorkel diving, I knew there was plenty of time to reach the surface. As I left the bottom my suit snagged and water began to pour inside. On the way to the top I tried the lung and was surprised that air again came easily. Thinking the trouble had cleared, I headed back toward the bottom. But the air shut off again, and I returned to the surface. Later I learned that when a tank gets too low in pressure to give air in deep water it will still give a few breaths on the way up. The pressure against our chest is less near the top so less air is needed in the tank to inflate our lungs. I also learned that the half hour my 38-cubic-foot tank was supposed to last meant only on the surface. Underwater the time was cut in half at more than 33 feet.

"On the surface, I found myself with an empty tank on my back, a rubber suit full of water, and faced with a long swim through a heavy chop to get to my boat. In order to

64

get my head high enough out of the water for a breath, I had to tread water hard and lift the heavy tank partially above the surface. This was exhausting, and I was soon puffing like a steam engine. I couldn't jettison my weights because the belt was strapped beneath the lung harness. And my snorkel was on the boat. It had seemed a useless piece of equipment when I put on the lung, but before the swim was over I would have paid a thousand dollars for that little item. At first I could swim all right, but dragging the tank, plus a suit full of water, and a heavy weight belt was slow work. A couple of times the regulator got tangled in kelp and I strangled on salt water trying to get it loose. That was when I decided to try and get the thing off my back.

"But I couldn't get the harness loose. I didn't know anything about the slip hitch which is used now. My harness was fastened in the conventional manner and the tension against the buckle was too much for me to manage while I was swimming. I held my breath and sank beneath the surface while I fumbled with the knot. But the water-soaked webbing wouldn't budge, and by the time I kicked to the surface I was gasping and blowing like a marathon runner on his last lap. What was worse, the struggle to keep my head up kept me puffing and I couldn't rest. I tried rolling on my back to sink the tank underwater. But waves rolled me around and I swallowed a lot more water.

"My last ounce of energy was spent when I finally reached the boat. I was so tired that for a long time I just hung to the anchor rope and let myself dangle in the water while I rested. Then, when I tried to climb on board, I found a new trouble I had never faced before. No one was around to help and I had no boarding ladder to climb up to the deck. It was a 36-foot boat, but I had always been able to remove my weight belt and kick myself aboard. Now, with a suit full of water, the tank, and the weights, I couldn't make it. I had visions of hanging in the water all night.

"I rested a long time, then grabbed the anchor rope and

65

pulled myself as high as I could go. With arms and legs straining, I let myself swing like a pendulum, gave a mighty heave, and one foot caught up on the deck. It seemed that I dangled there for hours before I managed to get my other foot up. Then, little by little, I inched my body over the deck until only my shoulders were over the water. My arms and hands ached from the strain of holding to the rope, but, with one last frantic effort, I let go and grabbed for the deck railing. My fingers caught, and I slithered aboard."

Bill was lucky. He is a strong swimmer and had enough power in his arms and legs to pull himself out of a mess. Other divers were not so lucky, and several who ran out of air in heavy kelp couldn't make it back to their float or to shore. It was from such experiences that the basic safety rules for scuba diving evolved.

Anyone can take a lung underwater and get by as long as everything works as it should and nothing unusual occurs. But only the very young or very foolish believe that nothing can go wrong. The wise diver learns what he should do in case of trouble.

It should not be necessary to explain common sense rules such as: never dive head first into the water while wearing a mask; be sure the air valve is open on your scuba before jumping into the water; hold tight to your mask when in surf or entering the water from a height (it will be knocked off your face if it isn't held); and clear the edge of a pool or a boat with your tank when you jump into the water. Carelessness in simple safety precautions such as these has caused injuries. There are a number of methods for entering the water safely while wearing a scuba tank. It is sometimes awkward to walk down steps or a ladder encumbered with flippers, weight belt, and other paraphernalia, and it is easier to jump in from the edge of a pool or from the deck of a boat. Of course, never jump into water along a rocky coast or into any body of water unless you are absolutely sure there are no obstructions beneath the surface. If entering the

66

water from a height the scuba tank must be held down to prevent the impact from driving the regulator into the back of your head. The shock of impact can be reduced by spreading your legs wide in a running position before you hit the water. Another method is to somersault and land tank down, on your back; or simply fall backwards and land in a sitting position. But whatever method is used, be sure your diving companions are out of the way and that there are no boats, floats or other debris beneath you.

It is also a good practice to take inventory of equipment before leaving on a diving trip, and especially before entering the water. It is easy to forget to put on a necessary piece of equipment and, once on the bottom, it is often too late to return for it. Occasionally a diver can get into trouble by forgetting a simple piece of equipment.

A friend of mine ruptured both eardrums because he jumped into the water from a boat without his flippers. He was weighted heavily for steadiness so he could sit or stand motionless on the bottom in taking motion pictures. With flippers he had sufficient power to swim even though carrying heavy weights. But this day he saw an interesting fish and jumped into the water, forgetting he had not yet put on his flippers. Unable to stop his descent, he went down like a rock, and ruptured both eardrums on the way. Without a quick-release buckle on the weight belt, he would have been stuck on the bottom until someone came to his rescue. By dropping the weights, he bobbed back to the surface and was hauled aboard the boat.

But these are careless mistakes which can be avoided through use of a little caution and common sense. Other safety precautions, such as the slip hitch, must be learned from the experience of others, or the hard way, by trying to teach ourselves.

The slip hitch is simply fastening the harness with a loop through the buckle rings in place of a single thickness of webbing. It works exactly like a slip knot. The end of the webbing can be pulled with one hand to free the harness. Experience also taught us to wear our weight belts outside the lung harness. The weights can be jettisoned quickly. In this way, a diver can make himself buoyant and retain his air supply. But the most important rule we learned was the "buddy" system of diving. With scuba we are free and independent with nothing to tie us to the surface world. This is at once a blessing and a curse. Once we disappear from the sight of companions, we are completely on our own and must be able to extricate ourselves from any trouble by our own initiative. We cannot wait for help. If help is needed it must be close at hand and immediately available. When we dive alone, companions will not miss us until it is too late. Men have died a lonely death with companions a few feet away, on the surface. In addition to the safety it provides, sharing the fun and excitement of an underwater adventure with a buddy doubles the enjoyment. And it is always good to have a witness who can back up stories of your exploits and experiences.

We also learned to wear a snorkel with a lung. It permits us to rest on the surface with our face in the water after our tank is out of air. We carry a diving knife not for use as a weapon against sharks, but to cut away tangled lines or kelp.

Most of us prefer a scuba tank equipped with some type of reserve valve which signals a warning before the air supply is completely exhausted. The most common and most popular type is a spring-loaded valve which cuts off the air when pressure in the tank falls below 300 pounds. The valve can be tripped and we have an additional few minutes in which to reach the surface or get out of a tight spot on the bottom.

The ability to clear a mask of water became a necessary skill in scuba diving. Not only does our vision depend upon a clear air space inside the mask, but water inside covers our nose and interferes with breathing. It is possible to get

air from a lung with our nose in the water, but we must inhale softly, with very little exertion, or water is snuffed in
and causes strangling. Also, we must be face down or water
will run down inside our throat and be inhaled. As explained
in chapter two, a mask is cleared by blowing out the water
while looking upward to the surface. This skill, as well as
breathing without a mask over our nose, should be acquired
in the safety of a swimming pool before diving is attempted.
Placing your mask on the bottom of the pool, you should
be able to submerge, swim to it, put it on, and clear it of
water without returning to the surface. This ability will help
you avoid panic and tell you what to do if your mask is
broken or becomes lost. Often our mask is knocked off our
face and fills with water.

The early scubas were not equipped with check valves (nonreturn valves) in the mouthpiece to prevent water from entering the air hose. Every time we lost the mouthpiece while
submerged, the hoses filled with water. If this water was not
immediately removed, our air supply was cut off and we had
to go to the top. At first, we simply drank the water out of
the hose until it was clear, and we could breathe again. But
drinking a quart or so of ocean water, especially near a
harbor, is a sickening experience, and is not recommended
except in extreme emergencies. Experiments later disclosed
that it is possible to blow the water out. The principle is
similar to clearing a face mask. Water runs downhill even
when a diver is submerged. It is only necessary to swim in
a position that will place the regulator below the air hoses.
In most units the left hand hose (over our left shoulder) is
the exhalation hose. To clear the unit, we swim on our left
side with our head downward until water runs to the exhaust
valve. Then, blowing hard will force the water out. It is usually possible to breathe in this position even before the water
is exhausted, as all water runs down into the exhaust hose
leaving the inhalation hose clear. Of course, if the unit is
completely flooded, no air can be obtained from the inhala-

tion hose until some of the water has been blown out. To clear a flooded unit it is best to lift the mouthpiece as high above the regulator as possible. Increased water pressure on the diaphragm causes it to trip and a flood of compressed air blows everything out of the inhalation hose. Remaining water can then be cleared as described before.

Practically all of the present scubas have nonreturn valves installed in the mouthpiece which prevent water from entering the inhalation hose. With these we can always obtain free air no matter how long the mouthpiece has been exposed to water. All that is necessary is to put the mouthpiece in and breathe. Exhalation will clear any water out of the exhaust side from almost any position. But it is wise to learn, and practice, what to do in case the nonreturn valves should fail, or an air hose begins to leak. This technique allowed me to continue working on an important job after my inhalation hose was punctured.

We were filming in 50 feet of water when my air hose was punctured on a sharp projection. It was late afternoon and light would soon be too weak for shooting. The extra time required to replace the ruptured hose might mean an additional day at this location. The leak was small, and the hose filled with water slowly, so I signaled that we could continue with the film. When the cameras were not rolling, and sometimes even when they were, I cleared the air hose by rolling on my left side as I exhaled. In this position I could get a breath of air mixed with only a slight amount of water. But we finished the scene and the shots looked good, except that my body was continually rolling from side to side somewhat like a wounded fish.

Knowing how to clear a leaky air hose will give you lifesaving air and time to think your way out of a tight situation. This skill should also be acquired in the safety of a swimming pool. Remove the nonreturn valves from your unit and place it with your mask and weight belt on the bottom of a pool. You should be able to submerge, clear the unit

70

and put it on, put on your mask and clear it, and put on your weights, without returning to the surface. Until this can be done, a diver is gambling against the odds when he finds himself in trouble underwater.

Some recent types of scuba are equipped with but a single high-pressure hose leading to the demand valve which is located at the mouthpiece. In this type no air can enter the high-pressure hose as long as the tank is under pressure. The only water that can enter the system is in the immediate vicinity of the mouthpiece where the regulator is located. A simple exhalation will clear this water.

In deep water we must be prepared for the possibility of suddenly losing our air supply. An air hose can be ruptured or a regulator can malfunction at 200 feet as easily as in shallow water. It is then that early training and skill with our equipment gives us the confidence needed to keep our heads. In such a situation we must remember the law of changing pressures and the effect of expanding gases. There is no need for panic or even any hurry. We can rise rapidly through the water from depths of 300 feet and never feel the need to inhale. Expanding air inside our lungs creates internal pressure and we can exhale continuously throughout the ascent. It is almost as if new air is created inside our bodies and we feel no need to take a breath. The rate of rise should be as rapid as exhalation dictates, or about the same speed as a large air bubble. But exahalation must be continuous or we may suffer an embolism and never have a second chance to try it. Of course, a rapid ascent from deep water can subject us to the bends or other troubles, but these need not become serious if immediate precautions are taken. These are explained later in this chapter.

The cylinders of scuba tanks are filled with air compressed to pressures between 2,000 and 3,000 pounds. The purity of the air in these cylinders became extremely important when skin diving shops across the country installed high-pressure compressors for filling tanks. No standards existed as a guide, and the purity of diving air was a matter of individual judgement. As a result, divers began to suffer a wide variety of illnesses caused by contamination of their air. Some compressors used ordinary oil as a lubricant, without proper cooling and filtering. High pressure inside the compressor cylinder caused the lubricating oil to flash and created carbon monoxide, which was pumped into the diving tanks. Carbon monoxide is a poisonous gas when breathed on the surface. Under pressure its effect is magnified, and divers suffered from headaches, nausea, dizziness, and even unconsciousness. Lubricating oil also produced another, more insidious effect upon divers. If the oil was not completely removed, it accumulated as a coating over sensitive lung tissue and caused a type of pneumonia. Mineral oil is not absorbed or thrown off by normal body functions, and its effect is cumulative over a period of time. For this reason, air pumped into diving tanks should be as free from oil contamination as it is possible to achieve.

In some cases, compressors were installed so carelessly that exhaust gases were drawn into the compressor intake and pumped into the cylinders. Little imagination is required to visualize the effects of breathing such air. The diver usually becomes too sick to continue before he reaches a dangerous depth. Fortunately, the contamination can often be detected by the foul odor, and it is a foolish diver who goes under after he notices his air has a peculiar smell or taste.

The best skin diving spots are often isolated hundreds of miles from the nearest source of diving air, and many of us depend upon small, portable compressors which can be transported to remote locations. When using these, it is important to realize the danger of a contaminated air supply. Extra filters should be carried, and changed as often as necessary to insure clean air in the diving cylinders.

Standards for purity in breathing air have now been well established, and there is no excuse for contamination. The contents of the air should be posted in the shop, and the date the latest test was made. Pure breathing air for scuba is defined as air which meets the following specifications:

Minimum oxygen—atmospheric air
Maximum carbon monoxide—10 parts per million
Maximum carbon dioxide—300 parts per million
Absence of odors and vapors
Freedom from oil and impurities by passing 5 liters of air
    through a Whatman #40 filter

If a portable compressor is used for filling your own tanks it is a good idea to test the purity of its air by having a sample analyzed by a laboratory.

For a number of years it was argued that slight amounts of impurities in diving air would cause no harm. Each day, the air we breathe in cities is contaminated with smog, auto exhaust fumes, industrial gases, smoke, oil, and a host of other undesirable elements. Apologists for bad air maintained that if breathing such impurities every day caused us no immediate harm, an occasional breath of the same poison would do no damage underwater. These people overlooked the laws of partial pressure and the absorption of gases under pressure which cause even oxygen and nitrogen to become lethal to a diver. These laws explain oxygen poisoning, the bends, nitrogen narcosis, and a number of diver's illnesses that were difficult to understand.

The air we breathe is a mixture of gases consisting of nitrogen 79 per cent, oxygen 21 per cent, and carbon dioxide (CO_2) 0.03 per cent. After inhaling this atmosphere, we exhale, under normal working conditions, nitrogen 80 per cent, oxygen 16 per cent, and carbon dioxide 4 per cent. A certain amount of each of these gases is retained in solution inside our bodies. But in skin diving, the air we breathe is under pressure, each gas is absorbed more readily, and it has an entirely different effect upon our body.

Henry's law states that, at a constant temperature, a gas is absorbed by a liquid in direct proportion to its partial pressure. Dalton's law of partial pressure states that if the pressure on a mixture of gases is doubled, the partial pressure of each individual gas is also doubled. From this we see that, at 100 feet and a pressure of four atmospheres, our bodies and blood stream will absorb four times as much of these gases as when under surface pressure, because the partial pressure of each gas is four times as great. Even though the percentage of oxygen is still 20 per cent in air we breathe at 100 feet, our bodies absorb as much as if we were breathing a concentration of 80 per cent.

This absorption of gases into our body tissues is the cause of practically all the diver's illnesses. For example, 1 per cent of carbon dioxide in air at surface pressure has no apparent effect, and it can be safely breathed for indefinite periods of time. But this same air, under 100 feet of water pressure, can cause serious harm. The carbon dioxide is under four times as much pressure, and will have the same effect on our bodies as a 4 per cent mixture on the surface. Carbon dioxide is the gas which stimulates our breathing. When we are under exertion, an excess of CO_2 builds up inside our bodies and our respiration is increased. The normal amount of CO_2 in the air is approximately .03 per cent. If the partial pressure of CO_2 is allowed to build up beyond 2 per cent of one atmosphere, dangerous intoxication can develop and even loss of consciousness.

The same applies to oxygen poisoning. Below 33 feet, two atmospheres, the partial pressure of oxygen is doubled, and it is absorbed twice as readily into our body. When pure oxygen is used the effect can cause convulsions, muscle twitching, and a variety of symptoms, as well as the sudden blackout previously described.

The bends, caisson disease, or compressed air illness, as the symptoms are variously described, is caused by the absorption of nitrogen into body tissues. Oxygen inhaled under pressure is used up by body tissue and exhaled in the form of carbon dioxide, but excess nitrogen absorbed into our bodies

74

remains until the pressure is reduced. Nitrogen is absorbed slowly into joints, muscles, and fatty tissue of our bodies. The amount absorbed depends upon the depth of a dive and the length of time under pressure. In shallow water of less than fifty feet a diver can stay under for an unlimited time with no danger from nitrogen absorption and the bends. But in deeper water, if we are under long enough for nitrogen to become absorbed, it must be allowed to escape slowly, or the effect is similar to quickly opening a warm bottle of beer. Nitrogen bubbles form in our joints, muscles, and blood stream, and cause excruciating pain, often followed by death. By rising slowly, with decompression stops according to established tables, the nitrogen gradually escapes into our blood stream and is exhaled without doing any harm. The decompression tables on pp. 176-177 tell us the depths and time we can stay under without a need for decompression. But every dive must be planned in advance or we might get into trouble. In this case it is especially true that a little knowledge is a dangerous thing, as a friend of mine discovered to his regret.

In the early days of scuba diving we were told by enthusiastic salesmen that, with a single tank unit, we needn't worry about bends. A single tank of air simply wouldn't last long enough, they said, because the air was used up faster in deep water and we couldn't stay under long enough to need decompression. This was true as far as it went. But it didn't give the complete story and led a diver into trouble.

He was exploring the remains of *The Valiant*, an old wreck lying in about 100 feet of water off Catalina Island. But the 15 or 20 minutes his single tank gave him on the wreck was not enough time to suit him. His remedy was simple. Extra tanks were rented and taken along for additional dives. But no thought was given to the bends or a need for decompression. He believed that returning to the surface between dives would satisfy requirements, and release the nitrogen from his system.

Fortunately, he and his companions were working from a

75

boat equipped with radio or his experience might have ended in tragedy. The other divers used only a single tank for the entire day, but my friend used up three separate tanks of air. He had a wonderful time with absolutely no trouble until the dive was finished. He had changed clothes, and the boat was on the way home before the first symptoms of bends appeared. It started with some slight pains in his legs which he attributed to cramps caused by heavy use of his flippers. But the pain increased rapidly and spread to his elbows and chest. Soon they became so severe that he was doubled up in agony, and was gasping for breath. A radio message was sent to the Coast Guard and relayed to the U.S. Naval station in San Pedro. The symptoms were immediately recognized as the bends and a helicopter was dispatched to rush the injured diver to a recompression chamber. He required over 24 hours of recompression before he could be released, but he learned a lesson he will never forget.

The time needed for decompression depends upon the TOTAL TIME UNDERWATER DURING A 12-HOUR PERIOD. Time is measured from surface to surface, and depth is taken from the deepest point reached in any of the dives. If a succession of dives are planned, a watch and depth gauge are essential to determine the depth and to time decompression stops. Scuba divers cannot hang suspended from a cable while their dives and decompression stops are controlled by a tender from above. They are independent in the water, and must rely upon their own equipment and judgment for their safety. During a decompression stop in ten feet of water a diver hanging motionless becomes extremely bored, and ten minutes can seem like an hour. This boredom can usually be avoided if shallow water reefs are close by. The diver allows extra time to swim into shallow water and spends his decompression period hunting or observing in this fascinating area.

Commercial divers working in deep water have been familiar with nitrogen narcosis or intoxication since 1930, but it was something entirely new to scuba divers. The French describe its effect poetically as "raptures of the deep." It is caused by absorption of nitrogen and CO_2 into certain sensitive portions of our body. The effect on divers varies from one individual to another, and in the same individual from one day to the next. Narcosis is seldom experienced at depths of less than 150 feet, and usually not above depths of 200 feet, so it is commonly referred to as deep water sickness. It does no permanent or organic damage to the body, and its effect is no worse than getting good and drunk. But imagine a drunken diver, on his own, at a depth of 200 feet, and the danger is easily recognized.

Nitrogen is absorbed by fatty tissue such as the brain and spinal cord, far more readily than by blood and other tissue. For this reason, when great quantities of nitrogen are absorbed into our system, it affects our brain. The symptoms vary with each individual, and under the influence of narcosis, divers are as unpredictable and unmanageable as drunks. Their judgment is impaired, they have hallucinations, hear music or voices, their muscles refuse to co-ordinate, and they seldom realize that they are in any danger. The water world is a rosy, wonderful place, and they can do anything that comes into their befuddled minds. Some have refused to keep their air hose in their mouth, insisting that they are as competent as any fish, and they try to breathe water to prove it. Some become belligerent and fight off any attempts to help. But the most common symptom, and the greatest worry, is a complete lack of fear or judgment. It is then that the attraction of great depths becomes a siren song inviting drunken divers into the unknown abyss to their deaths. This fatal attraction provided Courtney Brown, a prominent diver, one of the most harrowing experiences of his diving career. His description of the incident makes interesting reading. This is his story:

"Beneath the surface Catalina Island is a steep underwater cliff, plunging sharply down into the Pacific. Rutted by twist-

77

ing crevices and jutting rocky pinnacles, the submerged terrain drops crazily into abysmal submarine canyons thousands of feet beneath the surface. At the edge of such a canyon I played a drunken game of tag with a diving companion that could easily have ended in our death.

"We were searching for a speed boat which had knocked a hole in its hull in shallow water, but had remained afloat until it drifted out from shore. We dropped an anchor near the spot and found the depth to be just under 200 feet. Armed with double tanks, a watch, and depth gauge, we went down to make the search.

"We had often worked in this depth before, and had no difficulty reaching the bottom. The anchor was resting in a crevice on a sloping bottom of white granite boulders. Reddish-brown gorgonias fastened to the rocks waved fan-like plumes with the gentle surge of passing swells. A field of purple sea urchins, their spines bristling like clusters of colorful pin cushions, created a bright contrast against the white face of the boulders. We fastened a guide line to the anchor rope and began drifting over the area in an ever widening circle.

"After several passes we were at the end of the guide line and over a section which plummeted straight down into nothingness. A gigantic chasm or crack in the canyon wall opened below us, its side forming a sheer cliff which disappeared into the blue depths. I thought, 'If the speedboat went into that, we can kiss it good-bye,' and I turned to signal my companion. To my amazement, he let go of the line and sailed down into the drop-off.

"For a moment I was too surprised to move. Then, when he didn't stop or turn, I went after him as fast as I could flipper. Luckily he was not moving fast. But before I reached him, a strange sensation of well-being overwhelmed me. All at once I wondered why I was so concerned. There was nothing to fear in this wonderful place. Below me blue water disappeared into the depths and invited me to go on down. My

78

companion stopped and looked up at me with a peculiar expression in his eyes. In my happy state of mind our friendship seemed a marvelous thing and I considered taking my air hose out of my mouth so I could tell him how I felt. He swam toward me and I watched unconcerned as he took out his mouthpiece and let it dangle in the water. He mumbled and mouthed bubbles in an effort to speak, but made no effort to retrieve his air hose. It was then that a warning flashed through my numbed brain. Watching the life-sustaining air gush from his dangling mouthpiece triggered an instinctive danger signal. Years of training told me that this was a silly thing to do while underwater. It had a sobering effect. Fighting against the drugging narcosis, and the desire to relax and enjoy its blissful invitation, I grabbed my companion and gave him back his mouthpiece. He smiled agreeably, put it in place, and headed downward into the abyss. What followed was like a nightmare.

"He broke free from my grasp and was almost out of reach before I caught his flipper and pulled him backward. Then he turned on me like a tiger and we fought furiously as I tried to force him into more shallow water. All the time my own mind was numb, and it questioned the wisdom of the struggle. But when I decided to give up and join him in a mad plunge into the depths, a warning voice deep inside my consciousness shrieked of danger. And I continued the drunken battle. Once he pulled my mouthpiece out and almost got away before I could return it. Had he managed to go much deeper the narcosis would have won. Its effect was becoming stronger with each passing moment and each foot of depth. Finally, his face mask was knocked off and he was blinded by the water. This gave me an advantage. Under his blurred vision the depths lost their attraction and he became easier to manage. He tried to breathe and strangled on some water, then grabbed me and threw his arms around my body in a display of drunken affection. I kicked strongly toward the surface and dragged him upward. We were even with

79

the anchor, when, as if by magic, the narcosis left and he returned to his senses.

"We swam to shallow water for decompression, then surfaced and climbed aboard the boat. But even now, remembering the experience, it frightens me to think how close we came to a fatal ending. It was a sensation my companion described as a 'hopped-up' feeling that made him feel anything was possible. A person on the surface in a similar state of mind might try to walk across a busy freeway or jump from a speeding automobile.

"The amazing part of the experience was that all traces of narcosis left us as soon as we ascended a few feet. There were no aftereffects. The drunkenness cleared as in awakening from a dream. And at its onset there was no warning to put us on our guard. Narcosis is not like drinking which can be done in moderation. Once the symptoms set in, judgment is impaired and you are in danger of your life."

In shallow water the capacity of an air cylinder, and the time spent on the bottom are not extremely important. If we stay above fifty feet we need not worry about the bends and decompression. We can shoot directly to the surface when our air is gone and swim to our boat or back to shore. However, even under these ideal conditions, it is a good idea to know how long we can stay down and the direction of our travel. If a compass and watch are used, we can circle back toward our starting point before the air is exhausted, and save a long surface swim. In deep diving, when a double tank is used, it is vital that we know how long and how deep we have been under. Only then can we know if decompression is needed and the length of time we must stay at each stop.

The duration of a dive and the decompression stops are best planned in advance. Depth of water can be estimated from an anchor rope (with a margin left for safety). This information, coupled with the capacity of our tanks, will tell us if a stop is needed, and the time we must allow in shallow water. Most standard scuba tanks now have a capacity of 70 cubic feet when fully charged to a pressure of 2,200 pounds. Under average conditions this gives approximately one hour *on the surface.* But the time is reduced according to the depth at which air is consumed, as explained in Boyle's law of compressed gases. At 33 feet the time is cut in half, because the air is under twice as much pressure. At 66 feet we have one third the time, and at 100 feet a full tank of air will last only 15 to 20 minutes. Sometimes we must make a dive with a tank only partially filled, and must know how long it will last. By reading the pressure remaining in the tank and multiplying by .032 we have the number of minutes the air will last on the surface.

It is best to ascend slowly. Gases under pressure must have time to expand and be exhausted, or discomfort may be felt. Rising too fast sometimes causes momentary dizziness, but this should pass quickly. It also may rupture tiny blood vessels in our ears or sinus, or cause slight bleeding from the mouth or nose. This is ordinarily no more serious than a nosebleed in a child. But, if possible, it should be avoided, because some damage is sustained and in time scar tissue may be formed. A rule of thumb for a safe rate of ascent is: never exceed the rate of rise of your smallest exhaled bubbles. Of course, emergency conditions may dictate a necessity to break this rule. A diver out of air or in a state of shock cannot fool around with slow ascent. By exhaling continuously, a diver can shoot quickly to the surface from almost any depth. But, if in danger of the bends, he should either immediately be returned for decompression, or taken to the nearest recompression chamber.

It is extremely important to return immediately to the depth from which we ascended before symptoms of compressed air illness appear. Once the bends have set in, long hours must be spent in a recompression chamber. The bubbles that have formed, and which are causing the discomfort, must be forced back into solution. Then the pressure must be lifted gradually and carefully to avoid a recurrence.

Occasionally, when we are in deep water and out of sight of either the bottom or the surface, the weightlessness plays tricks upon our minds and we "get lost." There is no sense of up or down, and it is difficult to be sure in which direction we are traveling. Like a pilot flying blind, or a navigator in a heavy fog, we must rely upon our instruments and such things as air bubbles to maintain our sense of balance. Otherwise, vertigo can take charge of our direction and we may swim in circles. At times I have been positive my air bubbles were traveling horizontally and that my depth gauge was faulty. In this state it requires all of our past training and will power to follow the direction of the air bubbles back to the surface. Such vertigo is not encountered often, but when it is, we must rely upon knowledge and refuse to follow false leads from false impressions.

In addition to air embolism, bends, nitrogen narcosis, and oxygen poisoning, the absorption and expansion of gases in our system can cause other symptoms varying from a temporary discomfort to disabling injuries, depending sometimes upon the state of our health. For example, ear pain from pressure is a common symptom felt at one time or another by all divers. But, for a person suffering from a chronic middle ear infection, such pressure may cause permanent damage. Diving with a head cold may force germs into the middle ear and sinus and result in a serious infection. A simple cavity in a tooth has caused trouble. Air trapped inside the cavity, if unable to escape quickly enough, can cause a tooth to explode as we ascend to the surface.

Serious trouble is experienced when persons subject to heart trouble, asthmatic bronchitis, tuberculosis, blood pressure difficulties, and such illnesses try to dive. Skin diving is no more strenuous than many other sports but it does demand a certain amount of physical strength and agility. The great difference is that becoming ill or breaking down while underwater is far more serious than in the safety of your own home or even in a mountain camp. An injured diver must be transported to the surface, and then to shore or a boat, before he can be treated or allowed to rest. For this reason it is important to be careful of your diet before going into the water. Gas-forming foods or beverages should be avoided before a dive, and we should never go underwater if not feeling well. Expanding gas inside our stomach can cause distension of the bowels or even gas pockets outside the lining of the lungs. A physical examination by a doctor familiar with diving problems is the best insurance against diving injuries. Our health is too important to be jeopardized by skin diving if we have a physical handicap.

This chapter contains a frightening assortment of warnings and danger signals, but a novice diver actually will find little to fear when he first ventures into the world of fish. The hazards described in these pages and the technical information necessary to avoid them, were learned over a period of many years. Thousands of divers are underwater every day and incidents such as those I have used as illustrations are extremely rare. A diver in good health and familiar with the rules can enjoy skin diving all his life with very little risk. Knowledge makes it possible to avoid past mistakes, and tells us what to do in case of trouble. In skin diving, as in any sport, ignorance or carelessness is the cause of most accidents.

Today there is little excuse for a lack of proper training. Skin diving clubs exist in almost every section of the country, and most of them welcome newcomers to their ranks. A new diver can learn more in a few months with a club than he can learn in years by himself. Instruction on proper equipment for his particular area, and techniques in its use can be obtained from members of a club. They know the best diving spots, how to get to them, and hazards peculiar to the local situation. Instruction is also available from most skin diving stores, and a customer's safety is their business. Knowledge gained from a book gives an understanding of the problems which may be encountered, but it cannot create diving competence. Only practice and instruction can instill safe habits and give the confidence necessary for enjoyment of a strange environment. Also, skin diving is such a new sport that equipment is improving rapidly. Each season we are confronted with changes and advancements in design of old equipment, and introduction of new equipment which must be evaluated. A piece of diving gear, considered tops a few months ago, may now be obsolete. Through contact with members of skin diving organizations new equipment can be discussed and new techniques discovered which increase our ability to meet the challenge presented by the world underwater.

Food from the Sea—
Selective Fishing

A SKILLED skin diver should never starve as long as he has basic equipment and access to the sea. The oceans of the world offer an endless variety of exotic foods in the form of sea life, and most of it is fair game for the underwater hunter who knows what he is about. With mask and flippers we can penetrate one of the least known regions on the face of the earth, and our playground is an underwater jungle where the greatest abundance and variety of sea life exist.

Between deep water and the tidal zone lies a turbulent, shallow area inaccessible by any other means. Throughout the centuries this intermediate zone lay unexplored, and scientists could only guess at the mysteries it contained. Their studies were confined to sections exposed by receding tides or the quiet of deeper water in which a boat could be safely anchored and a helmet diver could work. But just beyond the breakers, where great swells surge and boil around jagged rocky reefs, and strong currents sweep through submerged canyons, is the wild and beautiful hunting ground of skin divers. In this region can be found a storehouse of sea creatures, from the largest to the smallest. In this zone tiny, helpless creatures seek shelter, and great sea denizens prowl close to shore in search of food.

The tidal zone is the spawning ground of the sea. In tide pools, nooks and crevices are teeming with millions of tiny

85

creatures hiding in the shelter of shallow water until they are large enough to venture away from shore. Permanent residents of the tidal zone are also a source of food for deep water predators. Animals and plants of this region have become acclimated to exist while exposed to air for short periods when the tide recedes. Their members include such delicacies as mussels, clams, crabs, and scallops. Beyond the area exposed by receding tides is a swarm of creatures existing upon the spawn and residents of the tidal zone. Myriads of rock fish lie waiting to pounce upon smaller victims. Lobsters and crabs crawl through cracks and crevices scavenging remains from another's banquet. Shellfish cling securely to the surface of submerged rocks, or are buried in the sand, their suction tubes straining microscopic organisms from the moving sea water. Flatfish, such as flounder, halibut, and rays bury themselves on sandy bottoms and lie camouflaged awaiting the approach of unwary prey. And into this zone from deep water come migratory game fish following schools of bait in the form of anchovy, sardines, or herring. All of these are the quarry of a skilled underwater hunter, wise in the ways of sea life, and familiar with his equipment.

Entering this wild and turbulent region beyond the breakers can present a problem to the uninitiated. Clearest water and the most beautiful submarine gardens are always found over a rocky bottom or coral reef. To reach these areas from shore usually means entering the water through surf rolling into the beach over partially submerged rocks. To negotiate such an area in safety we carefully select our point of entry, and leave the beach where wave action has the least force, or where a path can be found deep enough for swimming. We can float over obstructions without fear of being banged and bruised by wave action, but we never try to cling to partially submerged rocks. This is dangerous because they are covered with mussels and barnacles which are razor sharp and can cut severely. Also, we learn never to underestimate the power of huge surf. Riding heavy breakers over a sandy beach is exciting fun in a bathing suit, but becomes a different story when we are weighted down with heavy diving gear and breakers are crashing over a rocky reef. A strong surf creates a heavy surge over the bottom of shallow water, and can sweep a diver for long distances before its force is spent. An experienced diver can work in heavy surf, but he knows what he is doing from years of practice and training, and it should never be attempted by a novice. Even a moderate surf must be treated with respect, especially when entering or leaving the water. With experience, we learn to time our entrance between sets of breakers, and swim beyond the breaker line before a wave comes through.

Waves are caused by violent winds far at sea which whip the water surface to a frenzy and push it into mountainous peaks measuring as much as 100 feet from tip to trough. Great ocean swells are built by winds driving them across thousands of miles of water, and they race, unobstructed, until they crash against some distant shore. The greater the distance a wave is pushed by wind, the greater is its height and power when it reaches shore. The Pacific Coast has heavier surf than the Atlantic because of the greater expanse of unobstructed ocean.

Only the surface water is affected by a wave, and its action is similar to ripples when we wave a sheet of cloth. Water does not travel with the wave in any direction except up and down. Only the action travels as it ripples across the surface of the water. But near a beach a change takes place in the wave's construction. Shallow water applies brakes to the base of the wall and slows it down, while the upper portion maintains its original speed. This causes the top of the wave to crest as it climbs up and over the slowing water below. As the floor of the beach becomes more and more shallow, the wave reaches higher and higher in its climb until, finally, the entire structure topples over and it crashes with a resounding roar. The slowing action of the wave near shore creates an underwater surge which causes skin divers much difficulty. A large swell passing overhead moves the water toward shore with sufficient force to sweep a diver helplessly over the bottom when he is as deep as thirty feet. Then, when the swell has passed, he is swept in the opposite direction as the water surges out to meet the next oncoming swell. When working around sharp rocks under these conditions we keep our eyes ahead in the direction we are traveling, and we learn to hang on tight to the bottom until the force of a surge has passed.

It would be impossible to dive in shallow water when a heavy surge is rolling if it were not for the cushioning action of submerged rocks. When surge or current cannot pass through a solid object, the water piles up against it until its force is spent. Against a reef, this force creates a terrific surface turbulence and strong currents around the sides. In the center, near the bottom, things are relatively quiet, permitting us to dive with comparative safety. But beware of cracks or crevices which slice entirely through a reef. The entire force of a surge is concentrated in these narrow slots as water races through like a venturi tube. Before entering a crevice, cave, or slot beneath the surface of turbulent water, watch the action to make sure there is no opening at the other end to let the surge go through. Or better yet, confine your dives to quiet water until you know the area and can handle yourself under such conditions.

Underwater hunting is not confined to wild and turbulent areas where we must battle heavy surge and breaking surf. These conditions are stressed because of the hazard, and because the best diving on the Atlantic and Pacific coasts is in the clear water found off rocky headlands or over an offshore reef. Other areas in sheltered bays, coves, and inlets, or the waters off Florida, the Gulf of Mexico, and Puget Sound, Washington, offer excellent hunting, with little surf or surge. Here we have only currents to contend with, which usually maintain a steady flow in one direction, and are more easily recognized and handled.

Fishing with mask and flippers is a far cry from any other method, and far less effective in most cases. For a number of years, sports fishermen and conservation authorities were concerned about the impact this new method might have in reducing fish populations, and in some cases restrictive laws were put into effect. But in most regions, enlightened fish and game officials have now realized the ridiculousness of such conclusions, and the superstitious fears and prejudices of rod and reel enthusiasts and commercial fishermen have been allayed. But the battle is not completely won. Prejudice and superstition die a slow death and in some areas underwater hunting with a spear is still against the law. At this writing the Upper Keys of Florida are under such a ban, and only a few fresh-water lakes permit skin divers to hunt fish. In time perhaps the involved politics influencing decisions in these regions will be untangled and discrimination against underwater fishing will be lifted.

The fear and prejudice against skin divers stems from their use of spears. The word "spearfishing" is in a class with dynamite to a majority of sportsmen because of abuses in the past. Poachers armed with pitchforks waded into clear streams and rivers and hauled out salmon and trout by the wagon load. But a skin diver hunting underwater with a spear is in a different category. The ban against our sport may be justified for other reasons, but it has nothing to do with conservation. We must operate in water deep enough for us to dive, and we are underwater where the fish can see us coming, and have ample opportunity to escape. Experience has proved that, in a short time, fish in any region become spear-wise, and stay well out of range of an approaching diver.

Sea creatures are the most prolific in the world, and no method of taking them one at a time could ever have much influence on their numbers. One mature female herring spawns so many eggs each season that, if all were to remain unmolested until they reached full size the sea would be so full of herring we could walk across the water on solid fish. The

89

same is true of most fish. Nature has made them prolific to insure a continued supply of the species in the face of the terrible ravages of their ranks by predators. The tiny spawn of sea creatures is the animal plankton of the oceans which floats freely in all of the waters of the world, and serves as a source of food similar to grass and herbs on land. The off-spring of fish have little protection other than sheer numbers to insure that at least some will find shelter and survive to maturity. Man can upset this balance and deplete a species through use of poison, pollution, and certain types of nets which eliminate an entire population. But no amount of fishing with hook and line, or hunting with spears could have any effect upon the total number. Such things as food supply, contamination, and temperature changes have far more influence upon the fish which can survive in a body of water. Fish are cold-blooded, and can withstand little variation in water temperature from that in which they live. A sudden warming or cooling of the water will cause them to migrate with the current or perish. They are also extremely sensitive to chemical changes in the water, and a slight amount of contamination raises havoc with their numbers. One part per million of common detergent is sufficient to kill sea life, and our cities are dumping tons of such chemicals into the ocean every hour. Most large bodies of water are already supporting as many fish as the food supply will permit. They can easily reproduce faster than they can be taken with hook and line or by skin divers. When this is understood, the present prejudice and discrimination against underwater spearfishing may be removed.

Skin divers need not blindly accept anything which bites a hook. Their fishing is every bit as selective as any type of hunting, and it requires a great deal more skill. The common belief that spearfishing is as simple as shooting fish in a rain barrel is dispelled as soon as a novice goes under-water. Even the tamest fish presents an elusive target for an unskilled diver. We hunt in a fluid medium where everything appears to be in motion. The sea floor drifts back and forth beneath us as we float with the surge of passing swells, and we stalk a target which can disappear in a silvery flash the moment it is disturbed. Unlike hunters armed with high-powered rifles which can knock down game hundreds of yards away, our weapons have a range of only a few feet. We must stalk our quarry until we are almost close enough to touch it with our hands, and hitting the target is only the beginning of the struggle. We must hold it until we can return to the surface and haul it aboard a boat or string it on our float. With a fish of respectable size this can be an exciting and rewarding accomplishment.

Like hunters in any sport, only rank beginners shoot at everything they see or find satisfaction only in the quantity killed. An experienced diver takes pride in his ability to select his target among species which test his skill, and he often returns empty handed from locations filled with easy prey. The weapon used is also as important to spearfishing as it is to land hunting. A spearman who uses powerful weapons on pan fish is in the same category as a hunter using an elephant gun on rabbits. Again, stalking big fish with an under-powered weapon is as foolish as stalking grizzly bear with a .22 rifle. The weapon selected should be suitable for the type of game you are hunting, and in this it is wise to be guided by skin divers familiar with local conditions and the habits of underwater game in their area. Their preferences usually are the result of lessons learned the hard way, through experience.

Most skin divers and skin diving clubs agree that the true sport of underwater fishing is in holding our breath and diving with a snorkel. Except under special conditions or for a special purpose, the use of scuba for spearfishing is frowned upon. This opinion stems from the same source as the rules against heavy tackle in sport fishing. Greater skill and experience is demanded of the hunter, and, theoretically, the fish has a better chance. However, this rule is disputed in

91

many cases, as is the rule against heavy tackle, and for the same reason. It is true that, with light tackle, more fish get away. But authorities have established that a fish that has swallowed a hook will die even though he escapes the fisherman. And more wounded fish escape from snorkel divers than from skin divers using scuba. Also, some skin divers maintain that taking large fish with a light gun requires more skill than with a powerful weapon; while others insist that a quick, sure kill is more merciful than a wound which permits a fish to fight. So, underwater, we have the same argument between meat hunters and purists out for sport that exists in fishing circles throughout the world. But the bitterness and confusion exist because the rules and theories of rod and reel fishing are applied to underwater spearfishing. If we remember that skin divers are hunters even though their game is fish, most of the confusion is dispelled. No hunter would use a weapon designed to wound instead of kill, or judge the quality of his sport by the struggle of the animal to escape. Small caliber arms are outlawed for big game in most regions because of their tendency to wound. The same reasoning should apply to underwater hunting when the target is large fish.

The best type of weapon to use in any waters is one of the most controversial subjects in skin diving, and only personal experience will determine an individual's preference. But there are basic rules and techniques which never change and which we can learn from the experience of others.

Strangely enough, the crude hand spear of goggle fishing days is still a popular weapon. At first this was a broomstick or a mop handle armed with a heavy five-tined frog gig on the end. We learned that heavy tines are necessary for two reasons. First, lightweight barbs on the end of a wooden spear caused it to float horizontally on the surface and made it difficult to maneuver. Our target was always below us, and the spear had to be headed in that direction before we could submerge. The second reason involved the amazing strength of a speared fish. Even small varieties mangled light barbs as easily as paper and even quarter-inch tines have been bent like a pretzel by a large fish. Even with heavy tines, taking fish with a pole spear required a great deal of practice, skill, and luck. With no power applied other than the movement of our arm, the fish had a big advantage. Its reaction is four times as fast as a human's and our punch, retarded by the water, was like slow motion. Often a choice fish only tantalized us by moving or turning just enough to avoid the spear, and watched us, undisturbed by our best efforts. But sometimes we were lucky and caught one against a rock or on the bottom, where he couldn't bounce off the barbs. And we learned to increase the effectiveness of our punch by holding to the bottom so the thrust didn't drive us backward with as much force as the spear was driven forward.

Later, the spears were equipped with a detachable barb which penetrated more easily. The barb, secured with a line to the spear, was designed to detach after hitting a fish. With this improvement larger fish could be taken, as their strength was spent fighting against the line. They didn't tear themselves to pieces as when impaled on a solid shaft. But spearfishing was still ineffective until an ingenious skin diver rigged a rubber sling on the handle that would shoot the spear through the water with speed and force sufficient to penetrate the largest fish. Then underwater hunting became a science as we stalked our quarry through submarine canyons and underwater jungles and learned the habits of many strange creatures in the sea.

A skilled hunter can spot game when an untrained eye sees only the forest and the trees. And a skilled underwater spearman can spot fish when a novice sees nothing but water, rocks, and seaweed. Many species of fish have an amazing ability to change color and body markings to blend with their background so they are almost invisible. It is not at all uncommon for a diver to be surprised when an unseen fish jumps off the bottom a few inches in front of his eyes. A flounder placed on top of a checkerboard underwater would, in a few moments, take on the markings so clearly that we could play checkers on its back. When this type of fish is lying motionless on the bottom they are extremely difficult to see, and can usually be recognized only by their eyes or the outline of their bodies. Often we must approach very close and study the bottom carefully in order to see them at all.

We also learn where and how to hunt the different species. Not all submerged rock gardens or coral reefs are productive fishing grounds. Many bottom fish seek protection by hiding deep in crevices and holes, and few are found in terrain where such shelter is not available. When hunting such fish we look for a section of reef that is honeycombed with holes in which fish may be hiding. Other types of fish seek the shelter of kelp beds, patches of seaweed, a pier, or a wreck for their protection, and they can lead a diver a merry chase by weaving in and out of an underwater maze. Most of these are native to a local region, and their movements are limited to a relatively small area in which they make their home. Some have habits similar to land animals and take up residence in a particular cave or crevice which they defend against all intruders. Hunting fish in this terrain is mostly a matter of familiarity with the reefs, knowing where and when to look, and stalking close enough to fire before the quarry is alerted and escapes. Often a seemingly barren reef is like an apartment house whose occupants are all behind closed doors. By peering closely into the shadows of a dark underwater crevice we sometimes find an interior cavern teeming with sea life. Through experience, a skin diver becomes as familiar with the bottom of the ocean as with the streets and buildings in his town.

The greatest challenge to our skill are the migratory game fish which depend upon elusiveness and speed to escape their enemies. These are found in open water and are usually located by following flocks of feeding sea birds attacking schools of bait near the surface of the water. Beneath the bait we often find great, speedy game fish which are the fighters of the sea. Or they may be found at the edge of the intermediate region between the tidal zone and the sea as they pursue bait schools over shallow reefs. These fish are wary, fast, and powerful. Approaching within range of them requires skill and patience, and landing one after it is hit usually means a fight that is long remembered. A fish weighing no more than 30 pounds is powerful enough to drag a diver through the water at breakneck speed. If hit with a hand spear by a snorkel diver, it tests the stamina and endurance of anyone to "ride it out" before being dragged too deep or running out of air. If defeated, the diver usually loses his spear as well as the fish. Experiences such as this led to longer lines attached to the barb, and then to "break-away" equipment. The longer lines introduced additional hazards which the break-away partially eliminated. The hazard is best illustrated by an experience which resulted in ruptured eardrums for John Durgin, a prominent diver, and almost cost his life. Here is his story of the accident and the manner in which it occurred.

"A friend and I were into a school of rooster fish off San Carlos Point. This is a good fishing spot just north of Guaymas, in the Gulf of California. It sticks far out into deep water, with steep cliffs and big caves opening along the face where a skin diver might run into almost anything. The rooster fish were big in this school. Some of them weighed over 80 pounds. And they are fast and powerful in the water. Too strong for the spears we had. We couldn't hold them. It was a big disappointment. I stalked one for half an hour or more until I finally got close enough to hit it. The second the fish felt the spear it exploded in a burst of speed and hit the end of the line so hard it almost tore my arms from their sockets. All I could do was hang on. There was no chance to swim or try to turn the monster. I flew through the water as if I had hold of the end of a water ski rope. The fish was still going full tilt when I finally ran out of air

95

and had to let go. For all I know it is still swimming in the direction of La Paz.

"We lost a couple of spears before we changed our tactics. We figured that we needed a longer line on the barb to let the fish run while we came up for air. I attached about 50 feet of heavy nylon cord and wrapped it back and forth the length of the spear so it would pay out when the fish started to run. With this new rig, we went back into the water for another try.

"I was drifting on the surface when a big beauty cruised by about 20 feet below me. It was a perfect chance, and I sank quietly beneath the surface, being careful not to splash and alert the fish. Then I drifted down in a direction that would intercept him. This one was really big. His body looked longer than mine, and, as I drew closer, I could see his eyes watching me. But he showed no fear, and continued cruising lazily through the water, with only an occasional flick of the huge tail. Arching high above the silvery body waved thin strands of its dorsal fin which looked for all the world like a rooster's comb. I was about 10 feet from him, almost within range with my spear, when the big fish veered away as if sensing danger. I stopped swimming and hung motionless in the water—an old trick that sometimes arouses a fish's curiosity. And it worked. He circled slowly, then cruised in for a closer look. The spear point was only two feet from his body when I fired.

"The barb struck just behind the gill plate. The fish flashed away. The line started to pay out, and the next thing I knew I was jerked backward through the water with a loop of line around my ankle. Water roared past my ears. My mask flew off, and my foot felt as if it was being torn away. I tried to reach my knife and cut the line, but a rush of water tore at my body and held me helpless. Pressure increased and pain swelled inside my ears. Then I felt my ear drums go and I blacked out.

"I woke up on the beach with my buddy giving me artificial respiration. Both ears were bleeding, and I had a terrific headache, but nothing else was broken. My ankle had a deep groove where the line had cut into it, but the injury was not serious. My buddy explained that he had watched the entire action and had given me up for lost when the rooster dragged me out of sight. But luckily the shot had hit a vital spot and the fish was fatally injured. He saw the white body floating deep beneath the surface and went down more than 80 feet to get me."

After a few experiences such as this we were careful about the method of attaching long lines to our spear. We found it safer to carry extra line coiled in a ball and attached to the butt. A handle tied to the loose end could be grabbed after a big fish was hit. With a short cable used to hold the detachable barb, a fighting fish could be held until it was necessary to surface for a breath of air. Then we grabbed the handle on the safety line, let go of the spear, and headed for the surface.

Some divers attach their safety line to a float on the surface before diving. When a fish is hit they just let go and the fish spends its energy fighting against the float. But in currents, surge, or kelp, dragging a float over the surface while you are underwater is a nuisance, and most divers prefer free swimming, with no attachments to bother them.

The short range of hand spears was unsatisfactory for wary fish, and it was difficult to develop sufficient power to penetrate the really big ones with tough hides or heavy scales. For these a gun was needed, and a number of designs were attempted which met with dismal failure. We tried weapons similar to a bow and arrow and a crossbow. But the density of water slowed the recoil so much that arrows hardly moved at all. Then, since our hand spears were so effective, we tried attaching rubber bands to a tube and firing an arrow through the center. These met with better success, but wooden arrows were too light to carry any impact. A metal harpoon was substituted and the first "sling guns," or Hawaiian Slings, came into use.

These are still popular in diving areas where the water is clear and shallow, permitting use of a free shaft with no line attached. Several shafts are carried by the diver, as a big fish may require a number of hits before it can be landed. The shafts are 5 or 6 feet long, and made of $\frac{5}{16}$ to $\frac{3}{8}$ inch steel. They cause a fish to swim erratically so it can be pursued and hit with additional shafts if necessary.

When hunting in areas of limited visibility or in deep water, a line must be attached to the harpoon or it is easily lost. For this type of hunting several guns have been perfected which can be classified according to their source of power. The most common and most popular are rubber powered in which an elastic is used to fire a metal arrow. These are now available in any size desired, from short guns with light elastics for use on pan fish, to long guns with powerful, multiple elastics which are capable of penetrating almost anything that swims. Some are equipped with foot bars which utilize powerful muscles in the diver's legs to help stretch heavier rubbers. Others have a lever action to accomplish the same purpose, because, in this type of gun, the power and speed of the harpoon is dependent upon the elasticity and diameter of the rubbers and the distance they are stretched.

Other popular guns are powered by springs compressed inside a tube. These are also made in a number of sizes and lengths to suit an individual's strength and the size of game he is hunting. Like rubber powered guns, the range and impact of spring guns is determined by the size of spring and the distance it is compressed.

Compressed air, or CO_2 guns, are not dependent upon the strength of a diver's muscles for their power. With one of these, a harpoon fired by a child will hit just as hard as one fired by the strongest man. Most use a cylinder of compressed carbon dioxide or air to drive a heavy metal harpoon. They

98

develop tremendous power and can drive a harpoon completely through a large fish at a short distance. But their range is little greater than rubber or spring guns. The speed of the harpoon develops cavitation in the water which acts as a brake. Also, the concussion startles a fish in time for it to dodge if the distance is great enough.

One disadvantage of most gas powered guns is that they are loaded whenever the harpoon is placed inside the barrel, just as a rifle is loaded when a cartridge is in place. Most are equipped with a safety lock, but the protection of such a mechanism is no more positive than the safety lock on a rifle. No hunter will permit a loaded gun to be carried in an automobile or brought into camp. And no gas powered gun should have the harpoon inserted in the barrel except in the hunting grounds. In the air, these guns have a killing range of several hundred feet, and they should be treated as deadly weapons.

Unless a compressed gas gun is equipped with a gauge, fishing with it is an uncertain matter. It is impossible to know if a leak has developed or if the gun is out of gas. It is a little like hunting big game without knowing if a cartridge is in the gun. This can lead to some embarrassing, and sometimes dangerous situations, as the following incident will illustrate.

Hunting large sharks can be an exciting sport if the gun you are using is powerful enough. With Courtney Brown, I was hunting grouper in the Caribbean and noticed that the blast of compressed gas from the muzzle of a CO_2 gun had a frightening effect on big fish if they were close when I fired. But sometimes it had the opposite effect on distant sharks and brought them into the vicinity. I later learned that the natives occasionally used dynamite on schools of fish, and sharks were attracted by an underwater concussion like field hands by a mess call. My gun fired a solid steel harpoon ½ inch in diameter and 5 feet long, and it could split a 2 by 12 inch plank 100 feet away when fired out of the water. This power, plus the effect of muzzle blast, made me confident that I could take a killer shark with very little danger. I decided that the next one which tried to drive me away from my fish would get a big surprise.

We were over the edge of a coral reef which dropped off into a deep channel. The top of the reef was only 30 feet beneath the surface, and it was honeycombed with caves and holes providing perfect hiding places for grouper and rock-fish. We were snorkel diving and, because of the sharks, one of us watched from the surface while the other made his dive. Courtney was below me, and I watched him as he weaved in and out among brilliantly colored coral projections like a giant water bug. He pulled himself along the bottom looking into every nook and crevice for a likely target. As I watched him closely a flicker of movement drew my attention to deep water. I peered intently in the direction of the movement, straining my eyes to recognize a shape in the misty, blue infinity. Nothing could be seen and I started to turn my attention back to my companion. Then suddenly, over the edge of the reef, appeared a 10-foot tiger shark. He headed straight for Courtney. There was no time to signal a warning. I dived, and tried to head him off.

It was a race I was going to lose. The shark was too close. It would reach him before I was in range. I shouted, underwater, and the sound was muffled in a blurp of gurgling bubbles. But it was enough. The shark slowed, then turned in my direction.

I will never forget that instant. The shark swam slowly, straight at me. Its beady eyes were riveted on my exposed body, and the cruel gash that was its mouth looked two feet long. I knew that, inside, it was armed with double rows of razor-sharp teeth which could sever an arm or leg. But I was confident in the power and blast of my gun. I leveled the heavy harpoon and took careful aim. Then I waited until the shark was so close I couldn't miss.

It stopped a few feet out, then circled. I twisted, following with the point of the gun. Then the shark charged. I fired

100

The gun gave a weak burp. The harpoon dropped out. The shark loomed close, I jabbed with the empty gun barrel, felt the impact as it hit, and saw a blur of fast motion as the monster went sailing past my head.

The shark circled at a distance and I surfaced for a breath of air. But I felt awfully naked with a gun that wouldn't shoot, and watched, helpless, as it moved in for another try. But this time help was waiting. Courtney had seen the action and was now beside me in the water. As the big tiger sailed toward us, I said a little prayer that his gun wasn't out of gas. It wasn't. The harpoon struck the shark behind the gill plate. The safety line payed out. And, after an hour's fight, we took a hitch around the big tiger's tail and tied it to the boat. Investigation disclosed that my gun had developed a leak, and the gas pressure had escaped.

Gas guns have since been developed in which the compressed air serves only to drive a piston which propels the harpoon and the gas never escapes into the water, but is used over and over again. Some of these can be pumped up by a lever. Others must be filled originally from a compressor, or high pressure bottle. But these are more expensive than simple rubber or spring powered guns, and there is some controversy whether enough additional power is gained to justify the extra cost.

Spear guns are in use with a cartridge as power to drive the harpoon. These are machined as carefully as the action in a rifle, and they are an effective weapon if properly handled and cared for. At first it was considered dangerous to try firing an explosive charge underwater for fear the result would be similar to firing a rifle with the barrel immersed. If the barrel of a gun is plugged when it is fired, rapidly expanding gases cause the gun to "blow up." But underwater, the entire barrel is filled, no air space exists, and the shock of an explosion is avoided. The harpoon is started into motion slowly, similar to a rocket fired from the ground. All of the force is expended

101

out of the opening. But these have the same disadvantages of gas guns in that the noise tends to frighten fish. And a supply of cartridges must be carried into the water.

One of the most effective weapons developed for use on extremely large fish is the power head. This is an explosive head, fired by a cartridge, which is designed to drive a spearhead through a fish. They are used in place of the regular spearhead on the end of a harpoon, and will fit the shaft of most guns. Through a trigger mechanism, which must be cocked in advance, the cartridge fires upon impact and shoots the spearhead from the shaft. They are especially effective because all of the power is placed where it will do the most good, at the point of impact. Many types are so sensitive that they will fire if dropped through the water against a soft target. The spear or harpoon need only have sufficient power to carry to the fish. The power head does the rest. But these also have disadvantages and are dangerous enough that they should never be used by a novice. The disadvantage is that they should be used only on very large fish which are worth the trouble and expense of such a weapon. Two lines are used. One is the usual harpoon line attached to the shaft, the other is a longer line attached to the spearhead and which is used to play the fish. Each time a gun with a power head is fired both lines must be retrieved and recoiled. Further, if the shaft misses a fish and hits anything else, the head will fire. A lot of time can be spent digging spearheads out of rocks and coral unless the aim is accurate. Every power head should have an effective safety mechanism to prevent its being fired while carried on the gun. Otherwise it would be awfully easy to shoot your diving buddy simply by bumping into him while you are swimming.

A break-away line is almost universally used when hunting large fish in deep water. Otherwise it would be impossible to hold them or land them unless a lucky "kill shot" is made. Many divers also rig an inflatable float at the end of the line, which is triggered automatically if a fish runs to the end of the line. The float is inflated by CO_2 cartridges similar to those used in the life preserver called a Mae West. The safety line on guns is carried in a can or tube so it will pay out as the fish makes its run. Also in this tube a small parachute is sometimes carried which breaks out as the line starts to go and serves as a sea anchor to slow the rush of the fish. With this hook-up divers can take fish weighing over 500 pounds while using only a snorkel. If using scuba the diver can usually stay with a fish and "ride it out" so the float and parachute are not so necessary.

Spearfishing records are not recognized when fish are taken while wearing scuba. Also, many countries have adopted rules against the use of underwater weapons which incorporate power other than that derived from the skin diver's muscles. This outlaws gas guns, cartridge guns, and power heads for spearfishing in those countries. Among skin diving clubs, local, national and international competitions are held to determine championship spearfishing teams throughout the world. In these contests, no breathing equipment is allowed. All fish must be taken while holding the breath, and the challenge has led skin divers deeper and deeper in their efforts to win a championship. Depths of 60 and 70 feet are common among competitive divers, and many can hunt fish in water 100 feet deep while holding their breath. But diving deep or staying under as long as possible has introduced another hazard to which experts are most susceptible.

The danger involves the question: How long can a diver hold his breath before he loses consciousness? Each individual has a different capacity which varies from day to day. A number of divers can stay down as long as three minutes when not exerting themselves. But while hunting fish, one minute is a long time to hold our breath. A number of tricks can be employed to increase breath-holding capacity. Special diets of citrus juice and medication are followed to more efficiently utilize oxygen in our lungs. But the most popular method is hyperventilation before a dive. This is simply a series of rapid inhalations and exhalations taken as deeply as possible. The effect is to clear the blood stream of excess CO_2 and replace it with a maximum of oxygen. CO_2 is the gas which triggers a nerve in our brain and tells us when to take a breath. If this gas does not accumulate rapidly, the desire to breathe is weakened and postponed. But weakening the desire to breathe or delaying it too long is a dangerous practice. Our system can become depleted of oxygen and we may pass out without warning. Also, extensive training at holding the breath can reduce warning symptoms from CO_2 accumulation, and we can hold our breath past the danger point.

Competition divers, trained to a fine point, can hold their breath an amazing length of time at great depths. But often the balance between life and death is measured in a fraction of a second. A second too long in deep water and the diver loses consciousness while returning to the surface. In recent years, the lifeless bodies of some of the world's most outstanding divers have been discovered, floating in the water or sitting on the bottom, because they failed to allow enough reserve. This is a hazard especially to the expert, because his limit can only be determined after he has blacked out. The only sure precaution is surfacing with an ample reserve of air. But in the heat of competition, such safety measures are easily forgotten.

Few snorkel divers have any worry about holding their breath too long. Nature has provided most of us with a warning system which is so strong it is almost impossible to voluntarily hold our breath until we are in danger. Only those who practice hyperventilation excessively, or who have trained themselves to subdue the warning symptoms are in any real danger. However, a novice can pass out holding his breath if he tries inhaling pure oxygen to increase his diving time. Tests have been made in which divers have held their breath as long as 15 minutes after breathing pure oxygen. But this is extremely dangerous even under observation. CO_2 does not accumulate as fast as oxygen is depleted, and the diver often "blacks out" without warning. Unless he is immediately pulled to the surface, and artificial respiration applied, he will hold his breath forever. The desire to breathe has been eliminated.

Most spear fishermen pride themselves on their marksmanship and try always to place the harpoon in a vital part of the fish's body. This is the area near the head, and just behind the gill plate in the spinal column. If the spine is severed or severely damaged, a "kill shot" is made and the fish does not fight. If a "kill shot" is missed, there is sufficient bony structure in this area to prevent the barbs from pulling out. Any shot which penetrates bone will hold a fish, so any area along the spine is a good hit.

Practice with a gun improves marksmanship. With a new gun, I usually draw a traget on a sandy bottom and shoot at it from every angle until I am satisfied that the harpoon will hit where it is aimed.

Not all fish can be utilized as food. Every sea has some species which are poisonous and which skin divers must learn to recognize. This is not always easy. The poison is often due to a diet peculiar to a local region, and a fish which is good to eat in one area may be a poisonous variety in another. Also, the poisonous characteristics vary with the seasons in some species, making their flesh toxic only when certain organisms are present in the water. To be safe, it is best never to eat fish which are strange to you, and, in a strange country, be guided by the preferences of native fishermen. Their prejudices are not always based on superstition.

A skin diver need not depend on a spear or spear gun to obtain food from the sea. In fact, some of the most prized and delicious sea foods are taken with no other weapon than our hands. Along the east coast of America, great clawed lobsters are hunted by alert skin divers who know the area and the habits of these crustaceans. This is the lobster so publicized on restaurant signs that it is commonly believed all lobsters are equipped with claws. But these exist only along the New England Coast. The lobsters which abound in temperate waters throughout the world do not have claws, but are equipped with spines and feelers for protection.

The New England lobster is inclined to be aggressive, depending upon the strength of its claws to drive away an enemy. In hunting them a diver must be cautious or he may get his fingers caught in powerful pincers and suffer a painful wound. There are a number of techniques for grabbing them safely. One is waving our hands above the lobster until the claws are extended over its head. Then we quickly grab both claws and the lobster is defenseless. But be careful to get both claws. If one is missed, the diver may be the one who is caught. Another method is grabbing the lobster on the back, behind the great claws. But this should be practiced on lobsters out of water to make sure how far the claws can reach. These lobsters may be found hiding under rocks near the bottom, or in potholes in the mud of bays and coves. They are so delicious that divers often spend days hunting nothing else.

The spiny lobster, or seagoing crayfish, is abundant throughout the southern hemisphere, but catching them is something which must be learned. Their feelers are as sensitive as radar, and can detect a quick movement the instant it is made. They feed at night and hide in the crevices and holes of a rocky reef during the day. Years of dodging predatory enemies has made the spiny lobster wise, and his home is usually a crack or crevice extending deep into the interior of a reef. Or, if a shallow ledge, there are often several entrances through which the lobster can escape. They are located, sitting at the entrance to their home, with feelers extended to detect the approach of enemy or victim. To catch one, we must get our hands past the defense of the sensitive feelers before the lobster can scuttle into the reef. To accomplish this we take advantage of the lobster's curiosity. They have poor vision and cannot see our bodies. If we move carefully, the lobster is apt to try and touch us with its

106

feelers to determine if we are good to eat. But a quick movement, if detected, will cause it to jump as nimbly as a fly. We must feint the feelers to our mask and one free hand before we can hope to catch the lobster from behind. Even then, the struggle isn't over. The lobster can wedge its body so tightly against the rocks that it is impossible to pull it free. Only by shaking the lobster until it is confused or dizzy can its grip on the rocks be broken.

In some states and some countries spearing lobsters is legal and considered a fair sport. But in southern California, lobsters can only be taken by hand or in traps. Spearing them is not only against the law, it is looked upon by divers in the same light as spearing salmon with a pitchfork in knee-deep water. Southern California lobsters hide behind sea urchins with spines four inches long, and in crevices studded with razor-sharp rocks and coral, but they are taken by hand, and it is considered one of the greatest challenges in skin diving.

An abundance of food is available in shallow water for the skin diver who knows where to look and what to look for. We can take clams beyond the surf of sandy beaches where no clams are supposed to exist. We can find scallops in bays and lagoons and select the largest and most succulent for our meals. Over rocky reefs, we find rock scallops, rock oysters and, in some areas, the delicious abalone which is considered one of the delicacies of the sea. And there are recipes for cooking mussels and sea urchins, octopus and squid, which convert them into a tasty sea food dinner.

Abalone are a shellfish found clinging to rocky reefs in the submerged jungles off California and Mexico. They are large, ranging from 5 to more than 10 inches across the shell; they cling to the face of rocks with powerful suction, and it requires a pry bar to break them loose. They are hunted by both commercial divers and skin divers, for the meat is highly prized, and abalone steaks are a high-priced delicacy in restaurants and markets. Unlike clams and scallops, abalone have only one half their body covered by the shell. The other half

107

is a strong, tough muscle which is used as a foot for crawling over the rocks and which acts as a suction disc when the mollusk is threatened. The foot clamps the shell tightly to the rocks with sufficient strength so that heavy metal can be broken or bent in trying to pull them loose. Stories abound regarding the danger to divers from getting fingers caught by the abalone's suction and being held, helpless, until they drown. These are old wives' tales not based on actual occurrences, and almost every skin diver in the region has cut his eyeteeth diving for succulent abalone.

Abalone are not difficult to take. They are helpless except for the suction and the shell. But they are difficult to see and recognize. The shell is usually covered with barnacles and seaweed, so it looks for all the world like just another rock resting on the bottom. We learn to hunt them by peering close into crevices and spotting the fringe of feelers extending beneath the shell.

In other regions divers can search for rock scallops, a giant shellfish which also clings to the rocks of submerged reefs. These are much larger and more delicious than scallops found in bays and lagoons. Some weigh as much as 5 pounds, and only a few are needed to serve as a complete meal. On other reefs are oysters which can be harvested by skin divers armed with pry bars. They grow in clusters, are easily found, and taking them is only a matter of making the necessary effort.

On sandy bottoms beyond the surf of many coast lines some species of clam exists. These are harvested by clam diggers wading in cold water or working exposed stretches of beach during an extremely low tide. But they can be taken by skin divers at almost any time the water is clear enough to see. The siphon through which a clam strains nutrition from the sea exposes the clam's position to an alert skin diver. We learn to recognize the tiny mouth on the surface of a sandy floor as it sucks sea water to the shell buried in the sand below. Once a clam is recognized it is a simple matter for a skin diver to swim down and dig it out of the sand.

Also in some locations great delicious crabs can be caught as they scurry over the bottom. Conch shells can be hunted for their meat, and for their shell. And flatfish, such as flounder, halibut, and rays can be found buried in the sand.

The oceans of the world contain an inexhaustible supply of sea food which can be harvested by any skin diver who has learned what to look for and where it may be found. With a little training and practice to acquire the necessary skill, an underwater hunter could exist for years upon his harvest from the sea.

Creatures of the Sea

A SKIN DIVER entering the marine forests and submerged reefs of a water world must become acquainted with its inhabitants and learn which are enemies and which are friends. Life in the sea has grotesque shapes and forms, and it is easy to imagine ferocious characteristics which often do not exist. Man has an instinctive fear of the unknown and, until a skin diver becomes familiar with his environment, many of the strange animals of the sea will appear as fearful denizens. In order to fully enjoy the beauty and fascination of submarine gardens we must first learn to quickly distinguish imaginary dangers from actual hazards. Not only must the animals be detected among flickering shadows and moving vegetation but the type of creatures and its potential danger must be recognized.

In the early days of skin diving, the ferocious reputations of such creatures as sharks, octopus, eels, and barracuda had us in a constant state of nervous apprehension. The sight of one of these was enough to send us scampering to the beach. But, as our knowledge and experience grew, we learned that the legendary ferocity of most sea denizens is a myth. We found that we can swim and dive in waters infested with almost every type of sea monster, with very little danger. The voracious appetite of sea creatures is usually directed at each other and skin divers are seldom on their menu. But the possibility of attack does exist. Sea creatures are animals which react by instinct, and it is impossible to anticipate what they might do.

The size of an animal may be an indication of its power and appetite, but it does not tell its nature or the danger to a diver. Some of the largest are completely docile and can be approached in perfect safety, while some of the most aggressive are insignificant in size. We must learn their capability and treat the dangerous ones with proper respect and caution.

Sharks are the greatest villains of the sea. They are living fossils, prehistoric monsters which have remained unchanged through millions of years of evolution. They prowl all of the oceans of the world, but great man-killers are more prevalent in temperate, tropical waters. For many years it was commonly believed that man-killing sharks were found only in the open ocean far at sea, and an occasional foray into shallow coves and bays was a rare phenomenon. This belief was fostered by vivid descriptions of bloodthirsty attacks upon shipwreck victims when sharks appeared like magic in mid-ocean. We have since learned that, in some places, the same thing occurs in shallow water. A study of the shark will tell us why.

There is little reason for evolution to bring about changes in the shark's anatomy. Their efficiency as a killing machine is equaled in few forms of animal life. They are the scavengers of the sea which prey upon sick or wounded animals. They eat refuse, garbage, and carrion carried or thrown into the sea. They can devour and digest almost anything. Their bodies are unlike other animals'. The bones comprise a more primitive cartilaginous skeleton, and their skin is covered with tiny teeth instead of scales. These teeth, or denticles as they are more properly called, make the skin as rough as sandpaper, and a brush or scrape can inflict a surface wound on the tender skin of a human. The powerful jaws of a shark are filled with enlarged denticles, razor-sharp teeth capable of slicing through the toughest bone and muscle. Often they are triangular in shape and the top and bottom teeth fit together like the jaws of a powerful trap. In some species several rows of teeth exist, one behind the other, like theater tiers, and the front row is always in perfect condition. If a tooth is lost or broken, a new one moves up to take its place. The effectiveness of the shark's dental system is illustrated by the experience of a diver off Monterey, California.

He was diving with companions near Hopkins Marine Station when the incident occurred. Four of them were working from a small boat, hunting fish in water that was crystal clear. One man, who was aboard the boat repairing his equipment, looked up in time to see the dorsal fin of a great white shark moving slowly toward the divers in the water. He shouted, "shark," then rowed madly to the divers and began pulling them quickly from the water. Two made it safely aboard. But the third was underwater and could not hear their call. They waited for him to surface. Then the shark submerged. Nothing but water could be seen. They cocked their spear guns to go to his defense; then the diver's head bobbed to the surface a few yards from the boat. They called, but he paid no attention, and continued staring into the water. As the boat approached the reason for his silence became clear. Beneath the surface, two feet in front of the diver's head, were the wicked mouth and beady eyes of a tremendous shark. The two faced each other, staring motionless in the water. The diver, petrified with fear, clutched a bleeding fish close to his chest. The shark's fins rippled slightly. It was obvious the monster was on the verge of attack.

The oarsman quickly rowed the boat close to the diver's head. Four hands reached down, and heaved. The diver's body sliced upward. The shark struck. The diver kicked, and felt teeth rip his leg as he was jerked into the boat.

He was bleeding profusely and examination showed lacerations the full length of his leg from thigh to ankle. The razor-sharp teeth had begun to close above the diver's knee, and only the speed with which he had been jerked from the water prevented the loss of his leg. The triangular grooves cut into his flesh were deeper as they reached his ankle. The heavy rubber of his flipper was cut to ribbons, as if sliced with a knife. Later, the divers tried to make a deep cut with a sharp knife by sawing at the flipper but the rubber was too tough. Yet the shark had sliced through it with a single snap.

The sharks' equipment for locating food is as efficient as their ability to devour and digest it. Their hearing is so sensitive to underwater vibrations that they can detect the slightest sound from fantastic distances. Sound travels through the water at a rate of 4,950 feet per second as compared to 1,000 feet per second in the air, or approximately 4½ times as fast. Because of this speed, a shark can hear an underwater sound almost instantaneously. Sharks also have an acute sense of smell, and are attracted by an infinitesimal drop of fresh blood. In fact, blood attracts sharks from such great distances that one theory holds that the combination of fresh blood and salt water sets up an electrolysis which creates vibrations or sound. At any rate, a shark can zoom in on a wounded fish like a guided missile streaking toward a target, and fresh blood in the water serves as a radio beam which a shark follows as if guided by radar. The importance of this to skin divers can be seen from an experience I had in the Caribbean, and which has occurred to hundreds of divers throughout the world.

While filming preparations were underway, Max Pittman and I decided to spear a few fish for dinner. The water was crystal clear, with great visibility in every direction. We swam over a submerged reef where fish were abundant and I spotted a good sized grouper entering a cave about thirty feet below. From habit, I looked as far as I could see in every direction before starting down. Nothing was in sight. The water was empty of anything larger than the fish around the reef.

I sank slowly down toward the cave, lined up the gun on the grouper, and fired. The harpoon missed a vital spot and the fish began a furious drumming, beating the bottom with its tail. Blood flowed from the wound and gave the water a slightly crimson tinge. I started back to the surface, pulling the fish out of the hole and into open water. Then I saw it. A shark, 8 feet long, appeared. I watched as it streaked in, directly toward the wounded fish. Then another flicker of movement caught my eye and I turned my head slightly. Another shark, heading from the opposite direction, then another, from my rear, came in under me. Before I reached the surface, six sharks attacked that fish. They swarmed around it like hungry dogs after a bone. The fish was devoured in seconds and then they turned their attention to me. I hurriedly tried to reload my empty gun. Max joined me and we began to tread water, back to back, trying to keep them from getting behind us. Occasionally one would dart in close as if bluffing or intending to strike. This excited the others, and they moved in as if afraid they might be left out of an easy meal. Once I banged one with my gun, it was so close, and it fled as if it were actually hurt.

Gradually they drifted away and left us a clear path to swim back to shore. But it was an uneasy swim. We kept a constant watch in case they reappeared. All plans for hunting fish around that reef were abandoned. We ate beef the rest of the trip.

Similar experiences of other divers gradually gave us confidence. Hundreds of skin divers were approached by sharks, but none were attacked. Several theories developed, and a number of techniques which were supposed to frighten sharks away. Some claimed that diving directly at a shark would intimidate it and the shark would not attack. I have tried this and it works, part of the time. At other times it only seems to irritate an approaching shark. Other divers said that shouting into the water, splashing violently, and making threatening movements were effective defense tactics. These also work only on some species and on some occasions. But we do not know if the techniques caused the shark to leave without molesting the diver or if it simply was not in an aggressive mood at that time. I am convinced that the shark itself does not know what its intentions are before it acts.

At one time off Santa Cruz Island, in southern California, I was completely surrounded by Pacific blue sharks. I was diving about 100 yards from shore when I noticed a shark fin on the surface about 20 yards away. I started to swim to the beach, but other fins were cutting the water between the reef and shore. I looked around to see fins slicing the surface in every direction. I counted 25, and have no doubt that more were present, out of sight, underwater. Fortunately, I was working from a boat that was due to return soon. I trod water over a shallow section of reef and tried to watch in all directions at once. The sharks swam in a slow circle which drew closer with passing time. The surface fins drew within 50 feet, and individuals began to break away for closer runs. Then I saw the first one underwater.

It darted toward me from behind, but when I turned to face it, the shark veered away and disappeared. I was growing desperate when the boat sailed around the island to pick me up. I haven't the slightest doubt that, given time, one of the sharks would have summoned sufficient courage to make the first strike. That would have been a signal to the rest and they would have moved in like vultures over a dying animal.

The failure of sharks to attack divers gave rise to speculation that their ferocity was a myth. We believed that they would only attack a wounded, helpless swimmer, or one that appeared helpless to the shark. We reasoned that a swimmer on the surface, splashing and kicking, appeared like a wounded animal to a shark and invited attack. This is no doubt true. But our conviction that sharks would not attack a submerged diver who could see to defend himself was soon shattered. A skin diver in Australia was attacked and killed by a tiger shark. A boy in Monterey, California was killed by a great white shark. And others followed. Not many, considering the number of skin divers in shark waters every day, but enough to remind us that we were not immune. Some sharks do bite, and it is impossible to tell which ones.

Most shark attacks on skin divers have occurred in murky water when visibility was poor. In such conditions, a shark can zoom in on a wounded fish or a bleeding diver and strike before it is aware of the nature of its victim. Poor visibility also makes it difficult for a diver to keep a shark in sight. The majority agree that all marauding sharks should be treated as potential enemies, and kept under constant watch. Never try to run. A shark can swim much faster than a diver, and turning to flee only invites attack. They prefer to sneak behind a victim and take him by surprise.

Not all sharks are considered dangerous. There are some species which are found on the bottom, which divers actually take with their bare hands. Most of these are small species, but some are as large as many of the man-killers. A novice should not try to emulate these feats until he knows what he is doing. It doesn't pay to make a mistake. Even the tame ones can bite.

Another sea denizen with a fearful reputation is the octopus. They are bottom dwellers, infesting holes and crevices where they hide and await the approach of victims. Their tentacles are as strong as whipcord, and covered with a slippery, gelatinous mass. Along each of the eight arms is a double row of suction discs so powerful they can hold with a grip of death. The largest octopuses in the world have been taken from the waters of Puget Sound. One specimen, caught in commercial nets, measured 32 feet across its tentacles. Giants with a spread of 20 to 25 feet are not uncommon. It is these monsters that Puget Sound divers had to learn to deal with.

Experience with smaller specimens had convinced us that the danger of an octopus attacking was extremely slight. They proved to be shy creatures, only too happy to be allowed to escape unmolested. But we didn't know what would happen if a diver should accidentally put his hands on a really big one while groping among the rocks. It was taken for granted that a frightened or angry octopus would latch tightly to a skin diver and hold him helpless underwater until he drowned. We even speculated that one of the giants might attack. Supposedly documented evidence exists of such attacks, and the *Encyclopaedia Britannica* states that reports of their ferocious nature are well sustained. It is easy to imagine the apprehension of the first skin divers toward encountering one of these great sea denizens. Puget Sound divers not only encountered them, a member of the Puget Sound Mudsharks, a diving club, actually grabbed one, and it was no accident.

Jack Meyers had recently purchased a new harpoon for his speargun. His first shot with it missed a fish and the harpoon lodged in the body of a large octopus hiding inside a crevice. Jack's efforts to dislodge the harpoon failed. He was faced with a choice of giving up a $5 harpoon or fighting the octopus. He lost his temper, reached into the crevice, grabbed the octopus, and surfaced with octopus, spear, and all. Jack's octopus measured only nine feet, a baby by Puget Sound standards, but this taught skin divers an important lesson. The Mudsharks started a contest to see which of them could catch the largest one in bare-handed combat. As a result, octopuses with a spread of more than 20 feet have been taken, and an annual octopus wrestling championship is held which attracts skin divers throughout the Northwest.

Puget Sound divers are convinced that we need not fear the octopus. They grapple with them in caves, holes, and wrecks. The octopus is so frightened by attack that its only thought is to escape. It makes no attempt to hold on to the diver, even among the rocks. If it did, diving in Puget Sound would be a different story.

In their defeat of the octopus, skin divers have debunked the ferocity of one of the greatest villains of undersea fiction. Writers will have to search for some other monster to serve as guardian of sunken treasures.

The giant squid might serve this role. It is a cousin to the

117

octopus but more dangerous in habits, nature, and size. The squid has ten arms (rather than the octopus' eight), two of which are extremely long and are used like great whips to snare fast-swimming victims. Unlike the octopus, the squid is free-swimming and preys on fish for its food, while the octopus is a bottom crawler and feeds on shellfish and crustaceans. The octopus tires easily in open water, whereas the squid is a tireless and powerful swimmer.

Giant squid grow to monstrous proportions. Specimens have been found measuring over 60 feet in length, and they are believed to grow much larger. Their suction discs have tiny teeth around the edges which are capable of inflicting a severe wound, even if a victim escapes. Scars from these suction discs, larger than a saucer, have been found on the bodies of whales, evidence of titanic battles between these monsters in the depths of the abyss. An encounter with a giant squid would no doubt be a far different story from battling an octopus. But giant squid are believed to inhabit the depths and seldom venture into shallow water enough to be a hazard to skin divers.

Although whales are the largest animals in the world, they do not present a hazard to skin divers. It is amazing that their tremendous bodies are fed by some of the tiniest creatures of the sea. Their great mouths serve as a giant funnel to strain shrimp and plankton from tons of sea water. The mouth and throat are ribbed with thin baffle plates called baleen, which screen the tiny animals from the water.

Whales are known to battle with giant squid thousands of feet beneath the surface. One was found trapped in a transatlantic cable 3,000 feet deep, and it is not known how much deeper they can dive. For years it was a mystery how an air-breathing mammal could obtain such great depths without damage from a squeeze or suffering from the bends. But now it has been discovered that, as a whale sounds, its lungs are collapsed so no air space exists inside its body. During the dive oxygen is obtained from storage in the blubber and blood stream. This is also the reason why whales do not suffer from attacks of the bends. Air stored inside its lungs is not used during a dive, so nitrogen is not absorbed. Only pure oxygen from the blood stream, blubber, and muscles is utilized. In all of the nonhuman diving mammals, nature has provided a system for storing the needed oxygen which avoids diving illnesses encountered by man. Their blood stream carries over four times as much oxygen as ours and, during a dive, all circulation is diverted to their brain. No blood circulates to the muscles and bones to carry poisonous carbon dioxide or nitrogen. By diverting the blood to the brain, a greater supply is made available in the most critical area, and they can hold their breath for fantastic lengths of time. Even their desire to breathe is triggered in a manner different from that of a human. We can train ourselves to hold our breath until we become unconscious from a build-up of CO_2 poisoning. The desire to breathe in marine mammals is triggered by an oxygen deficiency as well as by an increase in CO_2. This double safety factor permits them actually to go to sleep while submerged. Their need for a fresh supply of air is triggered so definitely that they rise to the surface and inhale while still sound asleep.

Whales and porpoises have a unique method of finding and identifying objects underwater in total darkness or murky water. It is called echo finding. From their head they send out high frequency sound waves which act like a directional signal. The echo of this sound, as it bounces off an object and returns to the animal, tells the porpoise or whale what the object is, how far away it is, and its size. This detection system is so highly perfected that tests have demonstrated a blindfolded porpoise could differentiate an artificial fish from a real one when they were identical in size. It could also select a preferred species, and fish that was cleaned from one that was whole. The echo-finding mechanism in these mammals is as refined as our own hearing which permits us to identify certain sounds in a noisy room. It is not known how

119

many other sea creatures utilize echo finding in their search for food.

Skin divers have approached baleen whales and even attempted to climb upon their backs, and the whale has made no aggressive move. But again, we are dealing with an animal which reacts by instinct. Although a skin diver is not the natural food of a whale, he could easily be crushed by one sweep of the giant flukes or tail.

It is a frightening experience to be in the water with a monster as long as a five-story building. Once while I was diving off Point Dume I heard a sound like a miniature explosion on the surface behind me. I turned, and saw a giant gray whale spouting not more than ten feet away. Only its great head was visible. The huge body disappeared in a mist of foggy water beyond its head. The whale completely ignored me and I floated quietly, trying not to attract its attention. It filled its lungs, then slowly began to submerge. I watched it go down past me and it was like watching a freight train. It seemed hours before I saw the end. The broad tail moved slowly, but a strong current swirled me backward as if caught in a heavy surge.

Not all whales are harmless. Some have powerful teeth and love to use them so much they are known as killer whales. They are orcs, or grampus, and are the largest of the porpoise family, growing to lengths of 20 and 30 feet. Unlike baleen whales, which have no dorsal fin, the killer is easily distinguished by a great black fin which grows as high as six feet above its back. The killer is coal black on top, but has a white belly which can be seen as it porpoises over the surface.

The natural food of a killer whale is warm-blooded animals, such as seals, sea lions, porpoises, and other whales. One specimen was taken with the remains of 12 porpoises, 14 sea lions, and 1 dog in its stomach. No records exist of attacks upon skin divers by these ferocious animals, but there is little reason to doubt that they are dangerous. The killer's name is

120

derived from its habit of attacking herds of seals and slaughtering far more than it can eat, for the sadistic pleasure derived from killing.

A murderous orgy, typical of killer whales, was witnessed at Bird Rock near Monterey, California. A herd of fifty or sixty sea lions were gathered around the rock and in the water for the mating season. Suddenly the sea lions became quiet. All barking stopped. Many raised their heads high out of the water as if listening to something far off. Even the seals resting on the rocks seemed aware of approaching danger. They roused themselves and sat rigidly in an alert listening posture. But they made no noise. The rocks and cove were very close to shore and spectators had a ringside seat at the bloody action that followed.

The great black dorsal fin of a killer whale rounded the rock and entered the cove from the sea. The sea lions went rigid in the water, paralyzed with fright. A group of females clustered together with their heads underwater, flipper extended above the surface in a typical mating pose, were unaware of the approaching danger. These were the first target of the killer. He streaked toward them. His dorsal fin dropped deeper into the water until only the tip was exposed. Then he was among them and the seals exploded in frantic efforts to escape. Bodies flew out of the water in every direction as the killer engaged in an orgy of slaughter. Other killer whales followed the old bull into the cove, but seemed to be satisfied to act as spectators of his sport. Two females and two young bulls joined the mad old killer, but only he attacked.

The killers made several circuits of the cove and the sea lions were so frightened they made no attempt to escape. They swam or sat on the surface, their necks stretched high out of the water, waiting helplessly for sure death. A few climbed on the rocks but others, already on the rocks, were thrown into panic and jumped into the water directly in the path of the killers.

When the slaughter was over the bodies of a number of

121

sea lions washed ashore, their heads completely bitten off. No one knows how many others were killed in that bloody carnage, but spectators believe it could have been no less than thirty.

Killer whales are often seen far at sea as they prowl the oceans in search of baleen whales. The great whales are helpless to defend themselves against the vicious attacks of killers. They roll over on their backs and lie quietly as the killers force open their mouths and rip savagely at their tongues.

For years it was believed that killers rarely visited shallow water, and were no great hazard to skin divers. But this has proved false. Killers invade waist-deep water in their search for sea lions and several times I have seen their great dorsal fins above the surface between my diving position and the shore. Each time the monsters have completely ignored me and made no move which indicated an attack. I cannot say if they knew of my presence and paid no attention, or if they simply did not know I was in the water. But, with their sensitive hearing, it is difficult to believe that a skin diver could get by undetected. It is more logical to suppose that the killers just were not hungry or that skin diver was not on their menu that day.

There are other giants of the sea which can be classified with baleen whales so far as danger to skin divers is concerned. Manta rays are tremendous replicas of sting rays, but they do not have a stinger on their tail, and they feed on tiny organisms playing over the surface. Their great bodies sail into the air and drop back to the water with a splash that can be heard for miles. Some have a spread of over 20 feet, and weigh several tons. There is no danger of attack, but, if a manta should accidentally land on top of a skin diver or hit him with a giant wing, the diver could be pulverized.

Creatures with similar feeding habits are the basking sharks and whale sharks. These are true sharks and are the largest of their kind. But they are not ferocious and depend upon

122

tiny organisms to keep themselves alive. Skin divers have approached these sharks so closely that a photograph showed nothing but the eye, and the shark ignored the divers. They are docile creatures which need not be feared in spite of their great size.

Porpoises and seals cannot be so easily classified. We swim in their company without being attacked and their presence does not prevent us from entering the water. But they are like dogs and occasionally we run into one which is just naturally mean. There are no cases of attacks by porpoises on skin divers, and very few by seals or sea lions. Thousands of sea lions inhabit the Pacific from Alaska to Mexico, and almost every skin diver in southern California has come in close contact with them. The sea lion is a curious animal which loves to bluff a diver to see if he will run. The small ones seem to play a game, trying to come closest to the diver without hitting him. They attain a speed of thirty or forty miles an hour, and at this speed their wide flippers enable them to stop and turn instantly. It is a nerve-shattering experience to see several hundred pounds of seal streaking toward you at breakneck speed. Especially if the seal waits to slam on the brakes until it is so close only its eye can be seen peering into your mask.

A large old bull sea lion is the one which sometimes becomes dangerous. These should be avoided during the mating season and watched carefully at all times. On two occasions, these bulls have attacked divers. One diver was severely bitten across his back, and the other was grabbed by the leg. But two cases out of hundreds of thousands of sea lions and skin divers do not add up to great danger. Seals and sea lions are not generally considered a threat to a diver's safety.

The great barracuda of tropical waters reach lengths of over 6 feet, and weigh as much as 80 pounds. They are lightning fast in the water and their mouth is armed with long, razor-sharp teeth which can easily slice through the tough hide of a shark. Barracuda also have a vicious reputation and at first they were greatly feared by skin divers. They are attracted by bright, flashing objects moving quickly through the water and are known to strike blindly at such things. They are also attracted by blood or wounded fish, and skin divers in Florida and Caribbean waters often have their fish stolen by barracuda. But experience has proved their threat is more a bluff than real.

Barracuda will stalk us in the water, staying with us for long periods. They are a ghostly shadow sneaking through a watery background just within the range of vision. But, like a living needle, their slender bodies can dart with blinding speed to steal fish. Sometimes they drift slowly past our head, so close we can hear the gnashing of their teeth and see the snapping of the powerful jaws. For some time we believed that barracuda gnashed their teeth as part of a great bluff and that it was intended to frighten us out of the water. At first it succeeded. But then we learned that their fierce appearance and aggressive actions did not precede an attack. Scientists informed us that a barracuda must snap its jaws when moving slowly. The motion forces water through its gills in a volume needed for adequate breathing.

A few divers have been attacked by barracuda. But in each instance it was either a case of mistaken identity—the fish striking at a flashing bright object—or it was wounded or startled before it attacked. Although these great fish are capable of inflicting serious injury, they are usually not considered too great a hazard, and their presence does not prevent us from going into the water.

Another sea denizen with a ferocious reputation is the moray eel. These snakelike creatures infest the reefs in most tropical or semitropical waters and they are greatly feared by rod and reel fishermen. Along the coast of southern California, morays exist by the millions and reach lengths of 6 feet. In the Caribbean and South Pacific a larger species is encountered, with specimens taken measuring over 9 feet.

There is no question about the viciousness of a moray when

it is frightened or injured. I have never seen a more ferocious creature. They put on a display of temper and viciousness which has earned them a nasty reputation. On the end of a spear or a hook, they go berserk and will attack anything within reach, even themselves. The supple body can tie itself into knots which the moray uses to advantage in attempts to escape. I watched a hooked moray tie its body into a knot, then slide the knot up toward its head until a grip on the line was obtained. Using its own body as a lever, the moray pulled with enough strength to snap a 60-pound test fishing line. On other occasions I have watched them make a half hitch with their bodies around a spear shaft and use their tremendous power to pry themselves free of the barbs, or bend a steel shaft like a pretzel.

Almost every diver in eel waters sooner or later will come face to face with a moray. They hide deep in crevices where we are likely to look for lobster or shellfish. Looking through a mask at the wide open jaws and needle-sharp teeth of a wicked-appearing moray has sent many a novice skin diver scampering to the surface. They breathe with the mouth open so it always appears as though they are ready to strike. But if left undisturbed, the moray is inclined to keep the peace. They never go out of their way to strike unless they have been hurt. I have tapped them gently on the nose with an abalone iron and driven them away temporarily. One diver actually put his hand in a moray's mouth without being bitten. But it doesn't pay to make a fast move or grope blindly into crevices. A hidden moray can take a finger to the bone and, in soft flesh, they twist and turn until something comes loose. There is no need to be frightened at the sight of a moray, but they cannot be ignored.

Some of the most dangerous creatures of the sea are the most innocent looking. Nothing could appear more harmless than a beautiful jellyfish drifting aimlessly through clear blue water. But beware of the stingers hanging below the beautiful, pulsating body. In the Portuguese man-of-war and the

125

medusa types, enough poison is carried in nettle-like stingers to paralyze a diver, and even a slight wound is extremely painful. In jellyfish infested waters it pays to wear protective clothing and watch where you are going. Ascending into the nettles beneath a man-of-war could actually be fatal if the wound was near the throat or head. The venom is similar to cobra venom, and almost as deadly.

Other seemingly innocent creatures which can be nasty are the sea urchin and fire coral. The sea urchin is like a pincushion with brittle spines sticking up into the water. They infest rocky areas so heavily that they sometimes obscure the rocks to which they cling. Spines penetrating a skin diver's body usually break off inside the wound and are difficult to remove. If they remain, an infection is sure to develop which can become serious if not treated. Fire coral, as its name implies, is a stinging coral found in tropical waters. A brush with fire coral is similar to walking into a growth of nettles, but twice as painful. If diving in waters where it is known to exist, learn to recognize it and give it the clearance it deserves.

Sting rays can inflict a terrifically painful wound which, in some varieties, can cause unconsciousness. But they are a much greater hazard to bathers than to skin divers. A ray is not aggressive but strikes only in self-defense. They are found buried in the sand of bathing beaches where, if stepped on, they bury the stinger in the leg of the offending person. When walking in sandy areas, shuffling your feet will scare rays out of the way. A skin diver can see what is beneath him and should have no trouble with a sleeping or swimming ray. If speared, the ray must be handled carefully to avoid the stinger.

The most dangerous creatures in the sea are as tame as a house cat compared to a drunken driver. Diving in shark infested waters is much healthier than walking across a busy street. If sea animals were as vicious as their reputations, skin diving would have ended before it began. Instead, millions of divers throughout the world are in the water every day, and attacks are so rare that they still make headlines in the newspapers. The real hazards of underwater swimming are pressure, current, and ignorance. Every year we lose several skin divers because of pressure accidents and ignorance, while shark attacks occur less frequently than one per year. Man can kill animals or other men in a horrible fashion and it barely makes a ripple in the newspapers. But let an animal kill a man and it is a catastrophe broadcast across the nation. Perhaps it has something to do with our ego and sense of importance. Whatever the reason, if sharks and their ilk were the only hazard encountered by skin divers, the submarine world would be the safest place on earth.

8

Underwater Salvage and Treasure

Salvage means to save or rescue something which would otherwise be lost. In skin diving, salvage is retrieving anything from a pair of eyeglasses to a sunken ship. Or it can mean preventing loss or destruction through water damage. This includes every type of underwater operation from repairing a leaking dam to opening a plugged drain in a swimming pool. A diving operation to save a flooded city, or one to bring a lost toy out of a storm drain, are both salvage. The field is unlimited, and the term has been broadened to include underwater construction. Salvage divers are repairing piers and wharves, laying sewer pipe, surveying for new dam sites, and doing a host of other tasks as varied as modern civilization. It is obvious that volumes could be written without completely covering the subject, and that a chapter in this book can touch only a few of the highlights. But salvage diving is the field which excites the imagination and stirs the blood of trained skin divers. It is the area with the greatest need and in which little has been done. It also demands the greatest skill and training.

A skin diver engaged in salvage must not only be thoroughly familiar with his equipment and perfectly at home in the water, he must also be familiar with a wide variety of underwater construction and destruction tools. He must be a craftsman, an engineer, and have the ingenuity and imagination to pioneer in a field where few precedents exist and rules are made on the spot. Salvage work requires the use of tools underwater where often "up" is "down." Light equipment floats away and "falls" up to the surface, heavy equipment must be handled from above, and workmen float without the stability of gravity. Conditions are similar to those which will be encountered in outer space where satellites will be constructed from weightless objects. Perhaps underwater salvage with skin diving gear will prove to be the training ground for future spacemen.

The antigravity conditions expected to be encountered in outer space are so similar to those encountered by skin divers underwater that scientists are conducting underwater experiments to determine the effect on man of long exposure to conditions where no gravity exists. One such experiment, performed by Capt. Duane E. Graveline, an Air Force doctor stationed near San Antonio, Texas, illustrates some of the difficulties which must be overcome before space travel becomes practical. Incidentally, the same problems must be overcome before men can stay submerged for great periods of time.

Capt. Graveline spent a week in a 400-gallon tank clad in a skin diver's rubber suit, where he felt virtually no gravitational pull. After the experiment, the young doctor found that he could no longer tolerate gravity. His antigravity muscles and organs were soft and flabby, his bones soft, and his blood pressure was out of kilter. His movements were jerky and un-co-ordinated. He was removed to Wright-Patterson Air Force Base in Ohio where he was subjected to increased gravity forces in a centrifuge. His muscles and functions are expected to return to normal when his antigravity organs begin to work normally within a few weeks. The experiment illustrated that, unless artificial gravity can be provided in space, or some method of exercise devised to keep him in shape, the astronaut will suffer physically when he returns to earth.

Major salvage jobs require specialized equipment, specialized knowledge, and years of underwater experience. But skin diving equipment, with its low cost and extreme mobility,

129

has put profit into underwater jobs where none existed before, and opened an entire field of underwater exploration so new that no one can predict what the future might develop. Salvage itself is far from new. It has been practiced since the early days of history and maritime laws governing ownership of sunken objects have been established which are recognized throughout the world. These laws deal mostly with sunken vessels and are designed to protect insurance companies and shipowners from piracy, even after a ship goes down. Before salvage or treasure hunting is attempted for anything with important value, ownership should be traced and salvage rights obtained from the government which has control of the waters it is under. Many countries have strict laws forbidding salvage of sunken treasure, and confiscation can be expected after it is recovered. An object resting on the bottom of the sea has very little value and often salvage rights can be obtained at a small cost. But once the object is recovered, its value increases tremendously and rights may be costly to obtain.

An example of this occurred off the coast of Maryland, when the owners of the stranded and broken *African Queen* gave official notice that they were abandoning the 22,340-ton tanker and her cargo of crude petroleum. The *African Queen* went aground on a reef 9 miles at sea near Ocean City, Maryland. When skin divers read the notice of abandonment they assumed that the tanker and its cargo were fair game for anyone who cared to risk going after it. As a result great quantities of material were removed from the ship by skin divers who scavenged the wreck at considerable personal risk. Only then did the divers learn that an abandonment notice does not mean relinquishing title and the owners may still claim goods salvaged under such conditions. An abandonment notice merely frees the owners of responsibility for removing the wreck as a menace to navigation. The operation of the salvage divers is still clouded in a legal tangle and it will be some time before they know if the risk they took brought them riches in valuable cargo or if they may be prosecuted for taking another's property without permission.

Salvage can be attempted on a basis of speculation, the diver gambling that the value of his find will be great enough to warrant the cost of operation. But this is the exception to the rule and is usually confined to treasure hunting or souvenir excursions. More often the diver is hired and is paid a salary, or gambles on a percentage of the profits. As in any other occupation, the amount of work obtained depends upon a diver's ability and reputation. Salvage diving is similar to a doctor hanging up his shingle—the employers must believe he can cure their ills. This is the area which is open to promotion. Few people realize the advantages of scuba and the revolution it is causing in underwater work.

Conventional, hard-hat diving gear is heavy and cumbersome. Except under special conditions, it requires a boat, a crew, and a line tender before the diver can begin to work. Transporting this equipment to isolated areas is expensive and is not attempted unless the salvage has sufficient value or is important enough to warrant the expense. This is not true of skin diving. Our equipment can be quickly put into the back of an automobile, aboard an airplane or train, or even carried into the diving area on horseback. And if two skin divers must be present for safety reasons, the employer has two divers underwater at less cost than a helmet diver and tender.

Not only is skin diving equipment more mobile and cheaper to transport, the diver can work from shore in shallow areas, in swift currents, and over bottom conditions which make walk-around equipment impractical. Free diving is less apt to stir up a muddy bottom and limit visibility; obstructions such as weeds, stumps, and debris on the bottom can be floated over without difficulty. A search of an underwater area can be made in minutes by a trained skin diver which might take hours with conventional equipment. This is especially true on an uneven bottom where a helmet diver must be careful not to fall off an underwater cliff or get his feet wedged in a crack or crevice.

There are systematic methods for making an underwater search which insure that an area is completely covered and the looked-for object is not overlooked. Without some system, a diver has no sense of direction, cannot tell if he is being swept away by a current, and cannot make an intelligent search. The most commonly used are the circle and grid methods. The circle search is effective in murky or black water, with little or no visibility. The diver simply drops an anchor over the center of the area to be searched. In murky water a light line usually is tied to the anchor rope at a point near the bottom. The diver then pays out the line to its full length and starts searching the bottom in a circle determined by the end of the line. When he returns to his starting point he recognizes it by the bottom formation or a marker previously set down. Then a short length of the guide line is reefed in and the diver sweeps another circle. He should be careful not to take in too much line. Usually each circle slightly overlaps the previous one. If the object is not located, the anchor is moved and an overlapping circle started in a new area. By this method small objects can be located under almost impossible conditions. A wedding ring was located by a skin diver on the muddy bottom of a lake, and a pair of eyeglasses were found in the sandy bottom of Catalina Harbor. Both objects were located after only a few minutes of search by a skin diver using the circle technique.

The grid method is used to search for objects which are extremely valuable in a large search area. It is a square search which leaves no unswept corners. A wire or rope grid is laid on the bottom between anchors which form a square over the search area. Additional ropes or wires are either previously tied in place to make smaller, 6-foot squares, or they are snapped to the outer guides as the search progresses. Depending upon the type of bottom and visibility, the divers either search visibly between the squares, or use the grid as a guide for one hand while they sweep the bottom with the other. If the search is by feel, three feet are covered from one side of the wire, then the diver moves to the other and searches the remaining half. Two divers can work simultaneously, one on each side of the grid wire.

In comparatively clear water the grid can simply be ropes set a distance off the bottom between anchors to guide the diver as he swims. After a section is completed, the anchors are reset and another sweep is made. The same system can be used over a large area by towing a diver behind a boat as it is rowed between the anchors.

For sweeping an extremely large area in a search for sunken objects which can be recognized from a distance, the simplest and fastest is towing a diver behind a power boat. The pilot sets the course either by taking compass bearings, timing the heading during a directional run, or setting float markers in the water at the corners of the search area and running between them. A diver can be towed while hanging freely to a rope behind the boat, or a sea sled can be used which does not tire the diver and is more maneuverable. In some cases the anchor is partially lowered, and the diver simply sits or stands on the anchor during the search. But with this method the boat must move more slowly and the search takes longer.

Other methods of locating sunken ships or a shallow reef are to use sonar depth finders and underwater metal detectors. Depth finders will indicate a sudden bump or rise on the bottom which can be investigated by a diver. Metal detectors indicate the presence of large metal objects. But they indicate tin cans or rubbish as easily as a ship, so the area and bottom conditions determine if their use is practical.

During a search the diver should carry a marker buoy consisting of a flotation ball and a long length of light line. If the object is located but cannot be immediately removed, the marker will insure that it can be located again. The marker line can either be tied to the salvage object or it can be attached to a small weight carried by the diver, which can be dropped near the object.

These search methods, when utilized by skin divers, are proving especially efficient in search and rescue operations. Life guards, fire departments, and the Coast Guard are discovering that scuba is an efficient tool during water emergencies and are enlisting the aid of skin divers whenever possible. In the field of rescue, skin divers are proving that they can find victims under seemingly impossible conditions, and often succeed after all other methods have failed. Bodies have been recovered from ice covered lakes and ponds during subzero weather and at night. Victims of train crashes, automobile wrecks, and air crashes, where the vehicle has sunk into water, have been recovered by skin divers. And often rescue operations were conducted in the midst of flood-swollen waters of a raging, muddy river. Even earthquake victims were aided by skin divers called in when a mountain pushed a camp site into a lake near Yellowstone National Park.

Only a few examples of this type of rescue work can be given out of the thousands that have been undertaken, but they give some understanding of the capability of scuba equipment when used by experienced divers.

In Waterford, Connecticut, a small plane carrying three passengers crashed into Flat Rock Quarry and sank to the bottom taking its occupants to their death. The crash occurred at night in the dead of winter. Air temperature was below freezing and the quarry was covered with ice. Matters were further complicated by the fact that high octane gasoline from the plane's fuel tanks floated on the surface of the water, ready to explode into flames at the slightest spark. In spite of the extremely hazardous conditions, skin divers went into the freezing water of the quarry and recovered the bodies.

In Haverhill, Massachusetts, James Kimbrell fell into the swift current of the Merrimack River and was drowned. Police and fire fighters dragged the bottom in every direction, but found no trace of his body. Then skin diver James Cahill was called in from Danvers and within 15 minutes he recovered the body. Cahill's diving experience gave him a knowledge of river currents and their effect on a floating object, which enabled him to calculate accurately the position of the body. He went under, allowed himself to be carried by the current, and located the victim in approximately the place he had calculated it would be.

On the turnpike near New Castle, Pennsylvania, a huge truck and semitrailer crashed through the guard rail of a bridge and sank beneath the flood-swollen waters of the Beaver River. State police called to the scene of the accident couldn't see any portion of the vehicle or its driver, who was still pinned inside the cab. They called the Lawrence County Civil Defense Underwater Rescue Team and asked the skin divers to try and identify the semitrailer so owners and relatives of the victim could be notified. Visibility in the muddy waters was zero and the skin divers were unable to read the markings on the truck, but they established its identity by ripping off a door and bringing it to the surface. The truck driver was pinned so tightly by the wreckage that he could not be removed until the next day when a crane was called to the site and helped remove the cab.

In Canada, a log jam blocked the flow of timber down a swift flowing river, and owners were faced with the prospect of dynamiting a quantity of valuable logs unless the jam could be broken in some other way. The key log in the jam was beneath the swirling torrent of fast moving river water and could not be reached. Skin divers and salvage men, Laurie and Alex McCracken, were working in the area and offered to free the jam. Laurie attached a rope around his waist and was lowered into the river upstream from the jam. With torrents of fast moving water tugging and pulling at his body and threatening to sweep him into the maze of sunken logs, Laurie slowly lowered himself downstream until he reached the logs. Here the flow of water increased in velocity as it rushed through small openings. Laurie had a

135

cable with him to attach to the key log, but in order to reach it he had to work his way underwater into the center of the jam. Once his life line fouled and Laurie says he had a few bad moments as he tried to free it. In the blackness of fast moving, muddy water, he managed to work his way down to the key log and secure the cable to it. Then he pulled himself back to the surface and signaled Alex to haul him in. A powerful winch on shore pulled the key out from under the stack of logs, and the whole jam broke free, saving the lumber company thousands of dollars in valuable timber and lost time.

The use of skin divers for search and recovery is only beginning. Police departments of many cities are now training regular members of the force in skin diving, and in underwater search techniques. At one time criminals could safely dispose of the evidence of a crime by throwing it into the water. But the efficiency of skin divers and skin diving policemen is forcing them to look for safer methods of disposal. In Norfolk, Virginia, police officers were able to obtain a conviction in a robbery case after skin diving members of the force recovered a safe from the depths of Smith Lake. The safe had been thrown into the lake from a bridge after the robbery. While searching for the safe the officers also located and recovered an outboard motor that had been stolen three years before.

In Grand Haven, Michigan, skin diving members of the State Police recovered a sample case stolen from a pharmaceutical salesman, which contained dangerous drugs. The case had been thrown into Grand River after the robbery, but the officers were able to locate it quickly beneath the muddy waters.

In Los Angeles, California, police skin divers obtained a confession in a murder case after the criminal witnessed their efficiency in underwater recovery. He had claimed the gun used in the crime was thrown off the end of a pier into the ocean. The officers had him throw three objects from the same spot to determine the distance and direction before starting the search. They recovered the three objects so quickly in the murky water that the criminal gave up and confessed the actual hiding place. His comment was, "What's the use, you fellows would find it anyhow."

Another area of salvage activity is the exploration and scavenging of sunken ships which may still hold treasure or at least contain items with salvage value. Many people visualize an underwater wreck as if it were still afloat with everything intact. In reality it is like a modern apartment house turned on its side, the interior flushed out with a fire hose. Even a new wreck is such a shambles that finding anything inside is a major undertaking. In an old wreck that has been on the bottom for hundreds of years, nothing much is left except the skeleton. Tides and currents cover the interior with silt and sand. Often the entire ship is buried. Salt water is almost as corrosive as acid, and what it does not eat away marine organisms will devour. No human skeletons or clothing are found in ancient wrecks. Every trace of life vanishes into the sea, devoured by marine organisms or dissolved by the water. All wood is eaten by marine borers and sea worms. Metals, except those which resist corrosion, such as copper, silver, and gold, is corroded away until all that is left is a pile of junk. In exposed areas subject to violent storms and tides, even the junk is scattered and buried until often not a trace remains. But this dissolution takes time, and the skeleton of an old hulk will resist destruction by the sea for years, and provide a hunting ground for skin divers lucky enough to find it.

The fact that gold, silver, and jewelry do not corrode or dissolve into the sea has lured treasure seekers for centuries and is even more of an attraction today. The treasure of sunken ships is scattered over some of the wildest bottom in the oceans. It is buried by centuries of coral, sand, and debris and disfigured by attachments of marine organisms. But the treasure is so vast and the possible rewards are so great that hope of a lucky strike never dies. And a few are fortunate.

137

The shallow waters surrounding the Florida Keys were the setting for some of history's most virulent pirate operations, and the bottom is littered with ancient wrecks which went down with vast amounts of gold, silver, and jewels. Skin divers in these waters who know what to look for and where to look, occasionally surface with pieces of treasure. Along the Atlantic Coast, shipwrecks are a prime target for skin diving expeditions, and some make lucky finds. In the Silver Shoals, where an entire fleet of treasure-laden Spanish galleons went to the bottom, several skin divers have recovered a fortune in jewelry and gold, and no doubt other discoveries have not been reported because of legal complications. Off the coast of Mexico, in the Pacific, skin divers located the remains of *The Sacramento,* which went down with several million in gold. The gold has not been found, but the search continues.

Treasure hunting used to be an expensive undertaking. Expeditions with small fortunes tied up in boats, equipment, and crews were required. Skin diving has changed all this. Now a diver can go treasure hunting on a day's outing in a small boat, or even by swimming from shore. And it costs no more than any other diving excursion. Of course, once the wreck is located and salvage work begins, heavy equipment with suction hose and dynamite may be required to dig through the accumulation of debris. This is expensive work. Most divers prefer to look for loose baubles which can be scratched up from the bottom.

A skin diving group, in conjunction with the Smithsonian Institution and the National Geographic Society, are planning an exploration of the fabulous sunken city of Port Royal off the coast of Jamaica. Port Royal was the hangout for the most notorious pirates, such as Henry Morgan and Captain Kidd, during the heyday of the Spanish treasure galleons. It was destroyed in a violent earthquake, which dropped the entire city into the sea. Port Royal, if it is located, should produce a great many historical treasures and perhaps the strong-rooms of pirate hideouts will still contain treasure in gold, silver, and jewels.

A group of skin diving treasure seekers was organized into the Atlantic Salvage Company by John Potter of New York. They spent several years and all of their capital in a search for a Spanish treasure ship, *The Monmouth,* which was sunk in a naval engagement with the British in the Bay of Vigo, Spain. *The Monmouth* was not located, but a number of sister ships were, and the organization made its expenses by salvaging machinery and metal from the wrecks. Potter is now selling stock on Wall Street to finance additional searches for the payship. He believes the ship has been located under several centuries of mud which his crew is siphoning off. If the venture is successful, Potter's skin divers may recover $75,000,000 in gold, still resting in the bowels of the ship, and buried under 20 feet of mud.

Along the coast of wild, uncivilized sections of Yucatán is a graveyard of sunken treasure ships which have never been explored. Bob Marx, a Los Angeles skin diver, gained knowledge of these wrecks through extensive research into old shipping records. He visited the area in company with Dr. Nelson Mathison of Long Beach, intent upon searching for evidence of the wrecks and the possibility of recovering some of the treasure. He was successful beyond his wildest dreams. The ships were still on the bottom, as the charts and records said they were. And what is more exciting, the jewelry and gold and silver had not been recovered. Bob found exquisite jeweled crosses, necklaces, and rings worth thousands of dollars in metal and jewels alone. But their age and history made the articles even more valuable as artifacts and expensive souvenirs of another age. He was elated with his success and was dreaming of early retirement to a life of wealth and ease, when the Mexican government moved in and spoiled his plans. Marx had not obtained salvage rights to his treasure ships, and his find could not legally be retained. The Mexican government frowns upon what they consider grave digging, and they confiscated everything Bob Marx had recovered, with the exception of a few trinkets which they overlooked.

After this experience, and positive that even greater treasure was still on the bottom waiting to be uncovered, Marx went to local officials for permission to salvage future finds. He met with procrastination and delay, so he carried his tale and request to Mexico City, the capital of the nation. To officials in the national government Marx offered to continue diving if he were granted permission to keep only 25 per cent of his finds for himself. The major portion of the treasure recovered he offered to the government for its museums and historical societies. He was not refused. But neither was he given official permission. Instead, he was told that his proposition would be taken under consideration, and he would be informed of the decision later. Marx went back to Yucatán and waited. Meanwhile he continued to explore the area and, as he expected, uncovered more treasure. Marx says that it was uncanny how Mexican officials seemed to know when his dives were successful. If he found nothing during an excursion, he was not molested and saw nothing of officials. But if only one little trinket was recovered, the police were on hand immediately to confiscate his find. Several months passed with no word from the capital and no answers to his inquiries. After almost a year of delay, and a cat-and-mouse game with officials, Marx abandoned his treasure diving temporarily for other, more profitable adventures. The treasure of Yucatán is still resting, undisturbed and unclaimed, on the bottom of the Pacific. And it will probably still be there hundreds of years from now unless officials of the Mexican government change their policy or decide to conduct salvage operations of their own.

The amount of treasure still resting on the bottom of the sea staggers the imagination. The wealth of entire kingdoms went to the bottom during ancient wars when an invading army forced a government to flee. Treasure laden Spanish

140

galleons, filled with gold, silver, and jewels exploited from Indians in the New World, were sunk by raiding pirates, or crashed on unknown reefs. From the rich mother-lode country of California, fortunes in gold were accumulated and loaded aboard ships sailing to Eastern markets. Many of these ships never reached their destination, and their treasure is still unrecovered. Old shipping records show that a number of these ships are lying in shallow water off the coast of California and Mexico, waiting for some lucky skin diver to uncover their remains. Treasure seeking skin divers will do well to spend the time necessary in studying and charting the history of these ancient wrecks. Diving in their location is often no more difficult than visiting familiar diving grounds, and a pleasure trip may uncover evidence of undreamed-of wealth.

There are other treasures besides gold and silver. California divers near Monterey located an underwater deposit of jade, which could be salvaged. It has only a small value before it is carved, but it is treasure and highly prized. Others have searched in rivers and lakes where coins and rings are thrown in token of a changed life. One such place is near Reno, Nevada, the divorce center of the nation. Skin divers have retrieved a small fortune in coins and jewelry, tossed away by divorcees and superstitious gamblers, while their minds were befuddled by drink.

In the fresh water of inland lakes, salvage is a different story. Metal is not attacked as severely and wood is unaffected. Many items ruined by salt water retain their value when salvaged from fresh water. An example of this is sunken logs. The lumber industry has lost 5 per cent of the timber floated to the mills. It was too heavy and sank to the bottom where it has lain for a hundred years. This timber is in better condition than fresh-cut trees in the forest. Millions of board feet in top grade lumber, cut and ready for milling, is lying out of reach at the bottom of lakes and rivers. At the same time, lumber mills are abandoned on the shores of these same lakes because surrounding forests have been depleted. Armed with this knowledge, two enterprising skin divers retrieved sunken logs in Klamath Lake, Oregon, and made themselves a handsome profit during summer months.

In the Great Lakes a group of skin divers found a wreck with a cargo of whisky still inside. Some of the bottles were still intact, and the contents were reported in fine shape by those who sampled the merchandise.

In Puget Sound, skin divers enjoyed exploring the hulk of an old sailing ship, until they discovered the keel contained large quantities of lead. The next few weeks were spent in salvaging the lead, which was sold to enrich the club treasury.

A diver who worked as a greens keeper on a golf course in Arizona, used ingenuity to turn his diving to profit. Each year thousands of golf balls drop into golf course water hazards where they cannot be retrieved. This diver arranged contracts with a number of golf courses for exclusive rights to dive for the lost golf balls. As a result, he is driving an expensive car, has four divers working for him, and will soon be able to retire.

Finding an underwater object is only the beginning. It must be brought to the surface and floated to shore or put aboard a boat before it has any value. With small, lightweight objects, this is no problem. If they are too heavy for a swimmer to bring to the surface, a line from a boat can be used. If no boat is available, flotation can be improvised in a number of ways. A tire tube, tin can, or similar device will float a lot of weight. A tube is deflated at the surface and inflated under water after being attached to the object. A special attachment to an air cylinder can be used to fill the tube, or the valve can be held against an extra scuba tank. Tin cans must first be filled with water so they can be maneuvered beneath the surface. They are secured with the opening toward the bottom, and the water is then displaced by air. The opening in a can should not be sealed, or expansion of air as it ascends may cause it to burst. If no such float is available, a canvas sack will hold air long enough to take an object to the surface where it can be fastened to a more stable float. To put air into the sack the diver only needs to remove his mouthpiece and hold it over his head. Or he can let his exhalation bubbles be trapped beneath the sack.

Often an object to be salvaged is partially buried in sand or silt, and cannot be moved. Pressure can be applied to help remove it by attaching cans and filling them with air. The lift serves as a block and tackle to take the strain while the object is loosened with a bar or shovel. But the diver must stay clear. If the grip on the bottom is broken suddenly, the imbedded article will fly into the water with considerable force.

Extremely large and bulky objects can be raised by use of flotation equipment. Boats, ships, airplanes, and locomotives have been surfaced with no lifting power other than large metal drums attached in key locations. The drums are arranged in positions to float the object level with the surface, and then filled with air a little at a time. If the drums are properly placed, little damage will be done even to fragile objects such as airplanes. But, if carelessly placed and filled, the tremendous lifting pressure can tear a boat to pieces.

Using this method of floating a heavy bulky object, members of the Chicago Submarine Explorers managed to float to the surface and tow to shore a large Army plane which had crashed into Lake Michigan. The divers used a combination of inflatable rubber rafts, old tire tubes, and metal drums to raise the giant plane, but success was not achieved without difficulty. Several attempts were made which resulted in failure before the plane finally came to the surface to stay. The first try was made exclusively with rubber rafts which started the ship to the surface but burst under the tremendous weight. The second attempt succeeded in floating the plane, but when it was towed the floats became dislodged, the plane began to sink, other floats burst from the increased weight, and the plane went to the bottom again.

When the huge plane was finally beached, it was learned that the damage was too extensive to warrant repair, and it was given to the divers for salvage. The club is proceeding to dismantle the plane and market parts and pieces. Their treasury will be increased and all members will have had a wonderful time in the process.

The king of all boat racing events is the annual Gold Cup race, where giant hydroplanes compete. This is a race of unlimited power and tremendous amounts of money are invested in the hydroplanes which race at speeds exceeding 150 miles an hour. The Gold Cup event is held each year in the city of the winning boat. Last year, *Maverick* of Las Vegas, Nevada, raced and won in Seattle, Washington, and took the gold cup away from there for the first time in many years. In 1960, the Gold Cup is to be held on Lake Mead in Nevada.

All of this is simply to illustrate the significance of skin diver salvage. Recently the *Maverick* mysteriously exploded and sank. Skin divers located the giant craft in 175 feet of water and succeeded in bringing her to the surface without causing additional damage. Owners of the boat hope that examination will disclose the cause of the explosion. The *Maverick* was raised by sinking 55 gallon oil drums, attaching them to the boat and filling them with air.

Special suction pumps which work like giant underwater vacuum cleaners are used to remove sand and silt from heavy objects before they are raised. These same pumps are used to dig out an old wreck by divers in search of treasure. If the water and debris from the bottom is run through a screen, valuable articles will be caught and can be retrieved. On the same principle small suction pumps are used in underwater gold mining and in searching for coins and rings buried in lakes and rivers.

Skin divers have started a new gold rush in the mother-lode country of northern California and Oregon. Many of the gold-bearing rivers and streams were too deep to be worked successfully by old placer mining methods or gold panning.

These deep water sections are proving a bonanza to skin divers. Armed with a suction pump, digging tools, and a supply of air, the divers are mining enough gold on week ends to pay for a college education, and some are making a full-time living at it. Accurate figures on the amount of gold retrieved, and the exact areas worked, are not available. The divers who strike it rich are not making much noise, and they don't like publicity.

For the serious student, skin diving may be the means to future fame in his chosen profession. Scuba is rapidly becoming a valuable tool in the fields of archaeology, marine biology, and geology. Archaeologists are discovering evidence of ancient races deep beneath the surface of lakes and ponds. In Yucatán, a missing section in the history of the Maya Indians was uncovered by skin divers probing the bottom of Lake Amatitlan. Historical evidence in the form of ancient pottery, sacrificial vessels, and human skeletons were recovered under guidance of Stephan F. Borhegyi, director of the Milwaukee Public Museum. Dr. Borhegyi is not a skin diver, few scientists are. They must rely upon chance discoveries by untrained divers. Scientists who are also skilled skin divers can make observations on the spot and recognize phenomena the ordinary diver overlooks. In marine biology, diving scientists are discovering so much new information that previous theories must be discarded. So little is known of the underwater world that skin diving scientists must pass by a wealth of unexplained phenomena in order to carry out the primary purpose of a dive without becoming sidetracked. Work in this field is becoming increasingly important in conservation and pollution studies. Future operations may reveal that pollution is destroying a great deal more wealth than it would cost to provide treatment plants.

The world has an ever-increasing need for additional scientists and, if a scientist is also skilled in skin diving techniques, the opportunity for adventure and discovery is unlimited. He may accompany excursions to faraway places in

145

search of historical relics of past ages, such as a recent expedition to the Dead Sea, which disclosed evidence of lost cities described in the Bible. The expedition located remains of Sodom and Gomorrah, or evidence of their existence in the area now covered by the Dead Sea.

In Italy, a skin diver has discovered the ancient Etruscan city of Pyrgi on the Tyrrhenian coast, just north of Rome. Historical records describe the city, but only minor traces have been found on land. The Etruscans were a highly civilized race who ruled Rome from about 600 to 500 B.C., but little is known of their culture or their place in history. Under guidance of the Mediterranean Institute of Underwater Archaeology, skin divers intend to search the ruins in the hope that discoveries may enlighten historians about this ancient people. The expedition also intends to explore the sites of 20 to 30 additional ruins.

In St. Paul, Minnesota, scientists are excited about the possibility of new archaeological materials on the bottom of local and out of town lakes. A skin diver, Roger Nellessen, discovered an excellent piece of pottery in 40 feet of water on the bottom of Lake Phalen. The Science Museum of St. Paul is planning extensive diving operations in the lakes during the next few seasons in the hope of discovering additional artifacts which might add to their knowledge of ancient races and history of the region.

Skin divers exploring the shore of the Aegean Sea near the borders of Turkey discovered 41 sunken vessels, some of which dated back to the twelfth century. In an around the wrecks the divers discovered large jars, bronze and copper utensils, and other artifacts which are being put on exhibit in a special section of the fourteenth-century Turkish Castle at Bordum.

Near the city of La Paz, off the tip of Baja California, Mexico, skin divers from the Scripps Institute of Oceanography found underwater rivers of flowing sand dropping down the face of a submerged cliff on the edge of a canyon leading into the abyss. This moving sand is geologically important. Its discovery may explain some of the secrets of erosion along the continental shelves.

And so it goes. Throughout the world the search for knowledge, treasure, and salvage continues, and as long as people move over the surface of the water articles will be lost beneath the surface for skin divers to recover. Treasure hunting is rapidly becoming a science with much of the gamble and guesswork removed. Tools and equipment are improving, and new techniques are being learned which will enable skin divers in the future to perform salvage feats which are not now possible. But, even now, the field is unlimited, and opportunity awaits skin divers who know their business, and have the imagination to recognize situations where their skills are needed.

9

Hollywood Underwater

SKIN DIVING and underwater photography have introduced a new depth and range to the filming of motion pictures which have yet to be fully appreciated and exploited. The thinking of most producers is so obstructed by past experience and precedent that when Ivan Tors decided to produce an underwater television series the industry thought he was crazy. The experience of others had shown that even on an almost unlimited budget and flexibility of production in a major feature film, underwater photography was so difficult and expensive that the risk was hardly worth the effort. In the strait jacket of television production, with its limited budget and weekly time schedules, an underwater series was considered a fantastic venture. But fortunately, Ivan Tors is not easily swayed by precedent or the opinion of others, and he delights in doing the impossible. *Sea Hunt* was not only attempted, it proved that the judgment of its producers, sponsors, actors, and crew were correct by quickly climbing to the enviable position of one of the most successful series in television. The skepticism about an underwater program was so great that it was, at first, impossible to obtain a national sponsor. The program was syndicated and sold to local stations and local sponsors. Now that it is too late, national sponsors are crying for the show.

The prejudice against underwater pictures was not based on whimsey. Before skin diving became popular, and underwater photography became practical, motion pictures avoided underwater scenes like poison. The most simple scene required fantastic expenditures of time, money, and personnel. It was filmed either through a window in a tank, or from the surface through a "look-box." Usually a tank had to be specially constructed, and the look-box gave an endless series of problems in trying to hold it stable and keep the camera dry. All action was static, taking place within the confinement of the window. Lighting was difficult because the camera angle could not be changed. But the greatest problem was with the actors. Communication with the surface and the director was not possible, and all scenes had to be planned in advance. Once the action started, it was difficult to stop and usually ran through to the end even if an accident spoiled the scene. At its best, scenes shot under these conditions added little to a film, and seldom warranted the time and expense. Only set-up shots could be filmed. Immobility prevented the camera from showing marine life or submarine gardens as they actually exist.

Mobile underwater cameras and skin diving photographers have changed all this. The cameraman is underwater and follows the action through natural settings, with the entire submarine world as a stage. Directors also occasionally go beneath the surface where they can watch the scene develop and make corrections on the spot. In the hands of an experienced skin diver, the motion picture camera can take an audience beneath the surface into wild and beautiful regions any place on earth. In the comfort of a theater seat or in front of a television set in their own living room, millions of people can visit the submarine world and be introduced to its mystery, excitement, and adventure. They can see the beauty of submarine gardens off Catalina Island or a submerged coral reef in the Caribbean. They can explore flooded caverns in an underwater cave or descend into lakes in the craters of extinct volcanos. Without wetting a finger, an audience can search for treasure in a sunken galleon, ride the rapids of an underground river, and swim beneath the ice of a frozen lake. They can make the acquaintance of millions of grotesque sea creatures, fight battles with sharks and octopus, and see the struggle of tooth and fin as animals fight for survival in marine jungles. The camera can accompany scientific expeditions into savage, uncivilized countries in search of relics from the past, and the audience can share the thrill of discovering skeletons of virgins, sacrificed to the water god of the Mayas in the lakes of Yucatán. An entire new world is waiting to be recorded by the cameras of skilled skin diving photography teams who know what they are doing.

It is still true that making films underwater is far more difficult than on the surface. Conditions are so different that practically none of the old rules apply, and a whole new set of tricks and techniques must be invented to overcome the variety of obstacles. Not only must the crew be highly skilled in the techniques of motion picture production, some of them must also be skilled skin divers familiar with underwater conditions and capable of performing the hundreds of intricate and highly specialized jobs which go into film production. In *Sea Hunt,* the entire crew consists of competent skin divers who work as a closely knit team above and below the surface.

In any film the camera is the most important single piece of equipment. But in an underwater film, the cameraman is equally important. Lamar Boren is unequaled in this field, and he is responsible for the quality of underwater photography consistently obtained on our show. He has spent so many hours underwater, both with and without a camera, that he is more comfortable beneath the surface than he is on top. And this is necessary. When filming, a cameraman must concentrate entirely upon the action and the operation of his camera. He can't be fumbling with equipment or concerned about skin diving problems. His actions must be instinctive and only extensive experience enables him to control all of the changing factors encountered in underwater photography. He and the actors work in a fluid medium without stability or communication except through sign language. He encounters all of the problems of swimming underwater, plus those of a bulky, complicated motion picture camera.

The mechanism of the camera is protected by a heavy, pressure-proof case which Lamar Boren holds and maneuvers with his hands. No tripod is used, nor is it necessary. In the water, the camera is supported by the density, so it is almost buoyant, and it has much less tendency to jiggle than in the air. But the cameraman must be steady, even while he is swimming, or treading water. And sometimes this demands a diver who is as much at home in the water as a seal.

The underwater camera itself is an intricate mechanism which must be treated with care and carefully checked before and after each immersion. One drop of salt water inside the case could ruin the camera or the film. Changing film or reloading can be a delicate operation if, as is sometimes necessary, it is done on the pitching deck of a boat during a storm. The case must be thoroughly dried before it is opened, and extreme care must be taken that no water drips into the camera or on the film. All controls for the camera extend through the waterproof case, and adjustments are made while the cameraman is underwater. Even lens action is different. Objects appear to be one third closer than they really are and the cameraman must be sufficiently experienced to make corrections automatically which allow for correct focus.

Lighting is another vexing problem in filming underwater. When possible we film in clear water where direct sunlight is sufficient. But even so the light available depends upon the time of day and the turbulence on the surface. Smooth water permits sunlight to penetrate into the depths more readily than a ruffled surface. Wave action or whitecaps scatter and reflect the light back into the sky so a great deal of its intensity is lost. Because of this, a scene started in calm water often ends with a wind whipping the surface and the light intensity completely changed. Lamar Boren has the experience necessary to recognize these changes immediately

151

and make necessary compensations. Actors and crew are saved a lot of underwater time and work which would be needed to repeat the action. After four or five hours of underwater shooting, such ability is greatly appreciated by all concerned.

The demanding time schedule of a television series does not permit shooting underwater in color. Present color film requires not only extremely clear water, but also bright sunny weather. The film is too slow for shooting in the weak light beneath the surface on a cloudy day. In order to produce a new show every week, we must shoot in cloudy and rainy weather and during storms. Time simply does not permit the crew to sit around and wait for weather even if the budget did. But even clouds can cause trouble. We cannot see them coming when we are under, and the shadow of a cloud can change the light so drastically it completely spoils the film. When this happens, there is no alternative, the scene must be completely re-enacted.

Another reason for not shooting in color is that water acts as a filter in absorbing color from sunlight. Red does not penetrate much below fifteen or twenty feet, orange and yellow are filtered out a little deeper, and at thirty feet or more only blues and greens register on the film. In deep water these colors are also invisible to the naked eye, and I have followed a red fish as it swam toward the bottom and watched its color change from red to orange, through yellow, until finally the fish appeared blue-green. In deep water, a diving companion's face and hands appear a sickly blue-green, as if he were suffering from a violent illness.

Brilliant colors actually exist at great depths even though they cannot be seen. All that is necessary to convert the bottom into a riot of startling color is a powerful, artificial light which directs the color of sunlight into the depths. Perhaps in the future sensitive color film will be developed and artificial lighting techniques perfected which will make it practical to film an underwater television series in color. When this occurs, television audiences will be treated to the spec-

152

tacular beauty of deep water seascapes, as colorful as a botanical garden.

The buoyancy of water has both advantages and disadvantages for filming underwater. The fluidity of motion gives the camera mobility impossible to obtain on the surface. It can be moved smoothly in any direction to follow the action for almost any distance. Pan shots and dolly shots where the camera is moved in and out for a closer view do not require complicated expensive machinery to obtain the desired effect. Lamar Boren simply swims closer or moves backward while the camera is still running. But in some conditions, holding the camera steady on its target requires a lot of practice and underwater skill. If a surge or current is running strong, the water tends to push both camera and photographer off course. But Boren manages to continue shooting under almost any conditions, and no time is wasted while he adjusts himself against the movement of the water.

Our surface cameraman, Monroe Askins, is also faced with unusual conditions and must shoot from precarious positions not often encountered in motion picture photography. He finds it necessary to handle his camera on the bouncing deck of a boat being tossed by a choppy sea. Usually the boat is crowded with stage hands and the deck is a jungle of paraphernalia needed to make the film. Sound equipment, lighting fixtures, diving gear, and an assortment of props used in a number of scenes clutter the cramped quarters so it is difficult to find a place to stand or sit, yet the camera manages somehow to record the action without filming an extra's elbow, a stage hand's foot, or any of the items which would spoil the illusion of realism in the scene. Often the surface camera must shoot from beneath a pier or from a platform extended to the side of a pitching boat. Such scenes tax the ingenuity of the crew, and men with imagination, such as Mel Bledsoe, must improvise methods of getting the camera into position and holding it in place.

In one situation the sea was too rough to venture beyond

the harbor, and it was too risky to try and put the camera aboard. Waste of time was prevented when Mel stood neck deep in pounding surf while he hammered and nailed a platform into place on the pilings of a pier. At times the freezing water almost washed him off his feet or nearly sent him flying through the barnacle covered pilings. But Mel stuck to his job and the platform was completed. The camera was lowered into place and, from this position, scenes of action aboard a boat could be shot which appeared as if we were far at sea.

At other times the camera is set up on the beach where the action takes place over and around a rocky cove or point. Exposed rocks, covered with moss and seaweed, are as slippery as greased stepping stones. The cameraman, concentrating on the action, cannot watch his footing and is constantly in danger of a nasty fall. Once the tide came in while we were shooting and caught us all off guard. Camera, lights, and scene sets were inundated and scattered by the surf.

The entire crew of *Sea Hunt* consists of approximately 45 people, exclusive of the actors, and they are all dedicated to the successful filming of the series. Scenes are shot in two separate sections. Underwater scenes for a number of shows are shot at one time while on location. Surface scenes are shot at another time, and often a continuous action seen on the television screen is actually filmed as long as six months apart. A surface shot may be filmed several months before the crew leaves for location to film the succeeding underwater scene.

Because of the skin diving skill needed for underwater photography, not all of the crew is used for both situations. Only the technicians capable of handling themselves beneath the surface are a part of the underwater crew. These people must not only be skilled skin divers who are completely at home in the water, they are also highly trained technicians with a background in motion picture work which makes them tops in their department.

These people accepted the challenge of doing the impossible, and their dedication, co-operation, and ability has made *Sea Hunt* a successful series and proved to the industry that it is not only possible but practical to produce a television series with half the action taking place underwater. It was not easy. In most situations we were pioneering where no previous experience or precedent existed as a guide, and we learned by trial and error. Only the enthusiasm and tireless energy of each member of the team made it possible to overcome the variety of new problems encountered every week. Often we found it necessary to work 14 and 16 hours a day to meet a demanding schedule and make up for time lost because of an accident or dirty water.

Much of the credit for our success goes to Leon Benson, producer-director of the series. He has the patience of a saint as well as the dramatic instinct of a great director. Leon's eyes see the entire action in a scene and his judgment must analyze the effect it will create on the screen. He is alert to every sound and voice inflection and every movement on stage. His keen mind records the entire impression and interprets it in dramatic values as it will appear on the screen. For *Sea Hunt*, Leon learned skin diving and occasionally submerges to direct the underwater scenes.

Leon directs the action somewhat like a football coach directing the plays of his team. The scene is charted on the surface in advance, so each player knows exactly what he is supposed to do. The setting and camera angles are also planned ahead to obtain the most effective results. But often, the scene looks different underwater and does not go as planned. Then Leon dons skin diving gear and submerges to see how it can be done.

Bill Owens is production manager and it is his job to see that thousands of items are ready when they are needed. He assigns the various duties and ties the team together into a co-ordinated unit. An idea of the magnitude of this responsibility and its complications can be obtained from the fact that a minimum of ten separate shows must be filmed in one location before it is economically feasible to transport the cast and crew. This means that boats and accommodations must be arranged in advance so that the type of vessel needed for each show is available at the right time. Tanks, compressors, lighting equipment, sound equipment, diving gear, scene sets, and a thousand props must all be on location and ready when they are needed.

Jim Buxbaum is Ivan Tors' assistant and acts as story editor for scripts written for the show. He is a scholarly individual who loves to research new ideas and accomplishments in science. Jim is always coming up with new skin diving developments, recently invented by some enterprising skin diver, and surprising our audience. Occasionally this surprise takes the form of quick criticism by old-time divers who claim "it can't be done." But their criticism fades when, at a later date, the same innovation is carried in news stories or is announced in *The Skin Diver* magazine.

Harry Redman, in charge of special effects, and Max Pittman, property manager, make a team that is difficult to beat. From the story scripts and situations dreamed up by the writers, Harry visualizes settings which can be constructed to create the desired illusion. From the sets constructed by Harry's department, Max Pittman puts the ideas into execution and sees that they function as planned. Between the two of them, *Sea Hunt* has been able to successfully duplicate situations which it would be impossible to film. They have managed, on a limited television budget, to create effects usually seen only in major motion pictures with unlimited funds. They take the audience into a flooded storm drain, the wreck of a submarine, and countless sunken ships. Through their work, *Sea Hunt* has been able to film underwater caves, sunken mines, the interior of cargo holds, and submerged automobiles and airplanes. Apparently their ingenuity has no limit, and I firmly believe these two could create the illusion of almost any underwater situation. And that is the purpose of all dramatic shows—to create an illusion of reality on the screen which is dramatic, entertaining, and believable.

A motion picture crew is similar to a football team in that close teamwork and co-operation by a number of people enables the star to carry the ball. In football, the linemen run interference and throw blocks so one man can make the touchdown. In motion pictures, the crew run interference so the stars can tell a dramatic story. But in both cases, the performance of the star depends upon the ability and co-operation of his team mates. On *Sea Hunt*, I have been fortunate in working with some of the finest in the business. This teamwork is especially important to underwater action. Here we have no communication other than sign language and signals. The director can't tell us exactly what he sees and the cameraman can only cover a small section of water. If two underwater actors are unable to work together closely and smoothly, the scene drifts out of camera range, or worse, it becomes hammy and an obvious farce. Unfortunately, few professional actors are also divers so they are unable to perform while submerged. This obstacle is overcome by the use of doubles such as Courtney Brown, who is an integral portion of the show. He is not only an expert diver, capable of performing fantastic underwater feats, he is also thoroughly familiar with every aspect of skin diving and acts as technical director for the show. He is often the villain (underwater) or my buddy in a dive, and we have worked together for so many hours that we almost know each other's minds. Between Lamar Boren, Courtney Brown, and myself there has developed what amounts to a sixth sense which comes into play beneath the surface. Instinctively we feel what is required and what the other diver is going to do so we can swim into an underwater fight or dramatic situation without fumbling. Without this sixth sense and teamwork, underwater acting would be the most difficult I have ever attempted.

Acting is my profession. I have been on the stage or in motion pictures all my life and appeared as the star in a number of major productions. But *Sea Hunt* was my first attempt at performing underwater. It was a new experience which demanded that I learn a completely new set of techniques. Everything (except narration) is done in pantomime. Fear, excitement, or suspense must be demonstrated through body movement because voice inflection cannot be used. Even facial expression, the bread-and-butter of good acting, is limited by a face plate which covers my nose and eyes. My reaction to a situation is shown mostly through body movements, and these must be exaggerated to produce the desired effect. Under normal conditions, body movement underwater is slow and deliberate, as if performed in slow motion. Quick movements are difficult because of the density of the water and the fact that we are swimming freely with no support. These limitations make the teamwork and co-operation of Lamar Boren and Courtney Brown extremely important. The illusion we create depends as much on their ability as on mine.

A beautiful skin diver who often serves as a double for actresses appearing on *Sea Hunt* is Zale Parry, the lady diver who holds the women's depth record for scuba diving. Zale is not only a competent and tireless skin diver, she is also a capable actress and often appears in an important role.

A major difficulty in underwater work such as *Sea Hunt* is doing is the length of time we must spend beneath the surface on each shooting day. It requires an average of a day and a half to shoot the fifteen minutes of underwater action seen on each show. With a minimum of ten shows to shoot at each location, we must spend an average of five or six hours underwater every day. This demands that everyone in the underwater crew be in tiptop physical condition. Swimming underwater is exhausting work under the best of conditions, and in front of a camera, with underwater fights, rehearsals, and a variety of situations, it is even more tiring. For this reason, the location of underwater filming is extremely important. We must have warm, clear water in order to meet production schedules. Cold water, even with the protection of exposure suits, soon saps our strength and when we become chilled, we use air at a faster rate. We learned the lesson of clear water early in the series, and the experience almost sank the show.

We selected a location at the Coronado Islands near San Diego because of the grandeur of underwater formations and the beauty of the kelp beds. We arrived with a complete crew and the acting cast for several shows only to find the water invaded by a red tide and so dirty that shooting was out of the question. Assured by local divers that the situation was unusual and that the water would soon clear, we set up camp and waited rather than undergo the loss of time and money involved in moving to a new location. But the red tide was followed by a Pacific storm and milky water which caused further delay. It was fourteen days before we became convinced that shooting at this location was impossible and decided to move. The loss of time was equivalent to ten or twelve complete shows and set our shooting schedule so far behind that the entire crew worked night and day to make it up. An additional delay could have jeopardized our contract and perhaps sabotaged the series. After that we selected underwater locations insured against invasion from disturbances which might prevent shooting. This is one of the major reasons so many shows are filmed in the tropical waters of Nassau or in Florida's Silver Springs. The water is warm and its clarity is dependable. We can shoot without extensive and expensive delays.

We also find it necessary to shoot most of our action in shallow water above fifty feet. Working at greater depths uses air at a terrific rate and would subject the crew to danger from the bends.

While shooting is underway, Joe Gannon, another member of the *Sea Hunt* team, plays an extremely important role. The shooting script is our blueprint from which all scenes are shot. The story is never filmed in sequence and we are usually shooting more than one story at a time. Joe Gannon is a script supervisor who makes sure we are wearing the proper equipment for each separate scene. Otherwise, the audience might see a diver enter the water wearing a double tank and appear beneath the surface having magically transferred to a single tank. Or they might see an actor emerge from the water perfectly dry, or a swimmer change his style of flippers while moving from one part of a sunken ship to another. In spite of all precautions, mistakes of this kind do occur. Then we are swamped with letters and telegrams calling our attention to the error.

Near the end of a location stay, after the actors and crew have been subjected to hours and hours of underwater work for days on end, we tend to become a little punchy. In this state of mind it is difficult to remember which story is in progress and which sequence of events is in production. Sometimes I can't remember if I am supposed to be carrying an object toward the bottom or taking it to the surface. This happens to us all and it is then that the teamwork and cooperation help. What one actor fails to remember, the other usually does. And when none of us do, Joe Gannon is on the spot to cue us in the right direction.

Any number of interesting and exciting things occur while the *Sea Hunt* crew is handling underwater problems and no doubt they will continue to occur as we continue to film. Once, after thousands of dollars and a lot of time had been spent building a complicated set in ocean waters, we found that it could not be used. The set was a sunken ship stranded on a shallow reef and we had selected a spot with beautiful, natural scenery, ideal for the location. The crew arrived on the scene ready to shoot only to find the top of the set above the surface. In calculating location problems we had failed to consider the extreme change in tides at certain times of the year. The tide had receded, exposing our set, and all chances for filming were ruined until the set could be relocated at a deeper spot.

Another time, Lamar Boren's ears became infected with fungus so badly that it required fifteen or twenty minutes for them to adjust to the pressure every time he descended. To prevent an appalling loss of time, Lamar spent the balance of the day submerged, never surfacing for any reason. We even fed him lunch and snacks underwater so he could avoid the painful experience of pressure adjustment on his ears. This went on for several days until treatment finally eradicated the fungus and he returned to normal. In warm tropical waters, every diver in the crew religiously treats his ears with alcohol at the end of every day. If the ears are allowed to remain damp with warm water for a period of time, fungus is almost sure to develop. Treatment with alcohol dries out the water and acts as a mild disinfectant.

Often it is necessary to use artificial lighting on an underwater set. This requires heavy, insulated wires extending into the water and leading to the lights. Maintaining the exact intensity of these lights in the proper location, and having them ready at the right time is the responsibility of a highly trained and competent crew who take pride in their work. One time the lights went out during filming of an exciting scene and the crew scurried madly in search of the cause. The trouble was located underwater where insulation had been damaged and the wires exposed. It was quickly repaired and shooting resumed. But the lights went out again almost immediately. Investigation disclosed another damaged section which was also repaired. But when a third section went out, the director was on the point of accusing an efficient crew of using worn-out equipment. Tempers flared and an argument ensued which was becoming critical, when someone discovered a moray eel happily chewing on the wires. The eel was given a substitute to occupy its teeth, filming continued uninterrupted, and tempers returned to normal.

In California's Marineland, Lamar Boren was given a bad time by their pet whale, Bubbles. For some reason known only to Bubbles, she took a fancy to Lamar and demonstrated her affection by rushing playfully at him each time he entered the water. For a time Lamar enjoyed her friendship and the two entertained the spectators by cavorting around the tank. But finally Bubbles' demonstrations became so persistent they interfered with his photography. The great bulk of the whale, lumbering playfully around the cameraman, made it impossible for him to shoot. It was so disconcerting Lamar couldn't concentrate on his work. At any time a loving bump, which Bubbles considered delicate, might send him flying through the water with his camera. Or he might be sighting through the viewfinder and filming dramatic action, only to see a great eye peering into the lens as Bubbles tried to see what he was doing. All attempts to shoot were finally abandoned when a playful bump by Bubbles banged Lamar against the wall and almost broke his ribs. We returned and finished later, after Lamar's huge girl friend was transferred to another tank.

I am constantly amazed at the spirit displayed consistently by members of the acting profession. They simply refuse to give up and will agree to do almost anything that helps make a good show. A classic example of this was displayed by a girl who joined the show at Lake Mead. She was flown to the location in a seaplane. It was her first ride in such a vehicle and, as luck would have it, the weather was rough and extremely cold. To make matters worse, the cockpit was not pressurized nor heated, which made her hours in the air a miserable experience. Hanging tight to the small cockpit, her teeth chattering and her body freezing, she was tossed from one end of the sky to the other as the plane made its fluttering way through the storm. When it came time for the landing, she was already so frightened she was on the verge of hysteria. Looking down at the heaving, choppy surface of the lake as the plane descended she became petrified with fear which was not relieved by the landing. The plane hit the water and sent a deluge of icy water over the cabin which convinced her it had crashed. The storm-tossed surface of the lake bounced and jostled the plane so severely that, when it finally made the dock, she thought her safety was a miracle. This impression was increased by the sight of an ambulance leaving under emergency conditions.

Then, still shivering from the cold, and terrified by her harrowing ride, she was told: "Hurry and change into a bathing suit. You are going to jump into the lake from a boat." Dumbfounded, she pointed to the ambulance and was told, "That's a cameraman. He tripped, his camera fell on him and we think he broke his back."

The actress took one look at the stormy water, and fainted.

But later, when she had warmed up and decided we were not insane, she bravely boarded the boat and, with chattering teeth, plunged into the icy water according to the script.

Our shooting schedule does not permit us to film according to the weather. Often it is necessary to film tropical conditions in the midst of freezing cold, and the actors must perform in bathing suits while the rest of the crew are bundled into parkas. Once, in Florida, I was playing such a scene and became so cold that my teeth began to chatter like castanets. When it came time to speak my lines, my lips were stiff and I was shaking so badly that the words came out like stuttering machine gun fire. To remedy the situation and help me relax, the crew began to ply me with whisky. This worked for a while until everything began to seem hilariously funny. It was a serious, dramatic scene but my spirits were so gay and my mind so befuddled I couldn't play it. We finally stopped shooting long enough for me to warm up by natural methods.

Another problem plagues us often when shooting from a boat. Seasick actors and crew try to continue their chores between upheavals. This is one of the times when the old tradition of "the show must go on" is difficult to follow. I know, because at first I had the same trouble. At the time we had some spectators and guests aboard and I didn't want them to see Mike Nelson embarrassed by common seasickness. I tried to hide it and dashed for isolation (near the bow) whenever the urge swept over me. The sickness followed me underwater and it took a lot of maneuvering to time my breathing properly, between spasms. To make matters worse, the scenes were not going too well (probably the seasickness had a lot to do with it) and had to be repeated often. This meant going into the water and climbing back aboard the boat until I was completely exhausted as well as chilled to the bone. But we finished the show, and it wasn't until much later that anyone discovered I had been seasick.

Sometimes actors, hired through a casting office, present unexpected problems and excitement. We specify that, for underwater action or swimming shots with diving equipment, only actors with skin diving experience should be hired. But eager actors, looking for work on an exciting and successful series, often falsify their experience. We only learn it after they are in the water. Of course safety precautions are so thorough that the chances of a serious accident are practically eliminated. But an inexperienced swimmer can sometimes cause a lot of turmoil and confusion. One such case occurred at the entrance to San Pedro Harbor while we were filming surface shots from a boat. The action called for an actor-villain to go overboard while carrying a huge net. The actor had assured us that he was experienced with scuba and he was dressed with all equipment, including a rubber suit, weight belt, and tank. Right on cue, he jumped into the water with the net—and failed to surface. We waited, believing that he was simply staying submerged to make sure the scene was completed so he would not surface into the action. But still he failed to emerge. And then we saw a loose flipper floating on the surface. I had visions of his body, tangled in the net and sinking eighty feet to the bottom in murky water. Courtney Brown must have had the same thought because I was starting to dive into the water in civilian clothes when Court dived. He found the actor struggling in the folds of the net slightly beneath the surface. But Court reached him just in time. The actor had lost his mouthpiece and was sinking. It was quite a sight to see the two of them splashing over the surface with the net encasing their bodies. But the actor was game. He spit out a lot of water, caught his breath a minute, and was ready to continue. But we confined his acting to surface scenes aboard the boat.

The shortage of competent actors who are also skin divers is causing difficulty in casting. I hope that either more actors will become skin divers, or more skin divers will become actors so that in the future, we can choose from a wider field.

A few divers are critical of the *Sea Hunt* series because so often Mike Nelson is portrayed as a skin diver who works alone. They maintain that this violates the safety principles of buddy diving and is a bad influence on newcomers in the sport. These critics should keep in mind that *Sea Hunt* is not a documentary nor an educational film. Our excuse for existence is in dramatic entertainment and our purpose is to present an illusion of reality in dangerous situations which the public will enjoy and want to see. To obtain the objective it is necessary to have a story in which the character gets into serious trouble. Interest in the story comes from the audience's desire to learn how the character manages to outwit his enemies or extricate himself from a situation. To accomplish this, week after week, it is easier to provide situations of serious trouble for a diver who is alone than a diver with a buddy. Many of the situations in which Mike Nelson finds himself would not be possible if he always had a buddy standing by. This fact in itself speaks volumes in favor of the buddy system for actual diving conditions, and *Sea Hunt* goes a long way to illustrate the potential danger from going it alone. Also, theater audiences are conditioned to what is termed dramatic license in portraying the difficulties of a fictional character. How many people believe that my friend Hugh O'Brian, of *Wyatt Earp*, actually shoots as many people as his films portray? And how many people would try to take a gun away from a gangster because it is done so

165

easily by film detectives? In traveling throughout the country and talking with skin divers in every state, I find that the effect of *Sea Hunt* upon skin diving is beneficial.

Wherever possible we not only demonstrate but dramatize safety precautions and illustrate what can be done under emergency conditions. On film, my air hose has been severed, I have run out of air, and have been forced to "buddy breathe." In each case the audience learns that such situations, although dangerous, are not fatal. We demonstrate that experience pays great dividends in safety as Mike Nelson's knowledge and training help him escape from difficult situations.

Some of my most highly prized possessions are letters of approval received from diving clubs and diving councils throughout the country. A number of them have made me an honorary member of their organizations and have sent me membership cards and gold-plated plaques as tokens of their esteem. These I consider the finest compliment to my work in *Sea Hunt* that an actor can receive, and I am extremely grateful for the confidence and approval expressed by the organizations listed below:

Gold Plaques and Membership:
Skin Diver Magazine
Rhode Island Council of Skin Diving Clubs
Massachusetts Council of Diving Clubs
New England Divers
Illinois Council of Skin and Scuba Divers
Worcester Frogmen

Membership Cards:
Bay State Aqua Club
Seacraft Industries
Framingham Sea Urchins
Northeast Council of Skindiving Clubs, Inc.
Southbridge Skin Divers Club
Fort Pierce Reef Divers

As an actor, playing popular roles in major motion pictures over a period of years, I am accustomed to the usual run of fan mail. But in all of my years of experience I have never experienced anything to compare with the warmth and friend-

166

ship demonstrated by fellow skin divers. Thanks to *Sea Hunt*, I am now a part of a close-knit fraternity and I feel that I have friends wherever there is water.

This spirit of friendliness has been demonstrated in many ways. As an example, while I was playing *Guys and Dolls*, a skin diver in the audience stopped me as I was about to make a dramatic entrance up the aisle. I expected some comment about the play or an autograph request. Instead, to my complete astonishment, he said, "Mike, I'm having trouble with my regulator. After the show, maybe you can tell me what is wrong?" He had no interest in the play but came to visit a fellow skin diver.

Another time I was recognized by a Brooklyn cab driver who was also a skin diver. He was insulted when I tried to pay the fare, and said, "What kind of a diver do you think I am? Take money from Mike Nelson? Hah, you're one of the gang down here."

A sport which develops such fierce loyalty and such a strong feeling of brotherhood among its participants is a rare experience in a world of indifference and self-interest. I am happy that my two sons, Bo, 18, and Jeff, 10, are enthusiastic skin divers and can enjoy the same experience of close fellowship with the diving fraternity. They are also beginning acting careers and both have appeared in *Sea Hunt* episodes, so they too may get a comparison between fan mail and the friendly mail of fellow divers.

My daughter, Cindy, is only 6, but she is working on her diving in the hope of joining her brothers.

It looks as if my wife Dorothy may find herself in the midst of a webfooted family and she may have to take to the water in self-defense.

~10~

A Look at the Future

THE importance of underwater exploration to the future of civilization is not generally recognized, and, as a result, the United States is falling far behind other countries in the race for conquest and mastery of the submerged world. We know less about the ocean floor than we do about the surface of the moon, and present methods and equipment for oceanographic studies are as obsolete as the horse and buggy in a space age. Studies of the ocean bottom from samples obtained by dropping a container from the surface are as ineffective as a blind man trying to net butterflies. It is similar to a study of the earth's surface from samples obtained by dropping a container through the clouds from a space ship. Knowledge gained is from a small sample in an area the size of Massachusetts.

Science predicts a population explosion in the next few years which will put a tremendous strain upon the overtaxed and depleted resources available on land. Survival of this teeming population depends upon immediate measures to provide new sources of food, minerals, power, and water. In this race only two possibilities exist. One is conquest of outer space and transportation of resources from other planets. The other is developing methods and techniques to tap the endless resources of the sea. The need is so imperative and immediate that in the next few years we will witness submarine developments which may affect our lives as much as the industrial revolution or discovery of electricity.

The vast and mysterious world beneath the surface of the

sea holds promise of answering a great many of civilization's problems, the most urgent of which is food and water. Great industrial and population centers such as southern California, are now faced with a serious water shortage which threatens future growth. In other areas, entire countries suffer from starvation and famine because of arid conditions which restrict the growth of food. These countries are often located on the shores of a great ocean with an endless source of fresh water available simply by refining out the salts. Extraction of fresh water from the sea is now practical, and is more economical by freezing out the salts than distillation by boiling. Fresh water from the sea could convert these arid regions into fertile farm lands and comfortably support a greater population.

Only 2 per cent of the edible species of sea life are presently utilized, and an inexhaustible supply is available when mankind develops methods for extracting it. The recent descent of the bathyscaph into the Challenger Deep to a depth of 35,800 feet discovered fish and sea life existing at the bottom of the abyss, unaffected by tons of pressure. This discovery is extremely important as it proves that every cubic foot of sea water contains a potential source of food, and that the bounty of the sea is not confined to shallow waters. Experiments have already disclosed that fish and other sea creatures can be herded and husbanded like cattle on land. Nets of electricity perform the same service under water as fences, and future generations of skin divers will serve as undersea cowboys tending herds of fish. Electric nets not only prevent the desired species of fish from escaping and enable breeding controls, they protect the schools from predators and allow uninterrupted multiplication. The results will be fantastic. Fish are so prolific that if in a single season all the spawn of one species were permitted to reach maturity the sea would be so full of fish there would be no room for water.

Even more fantastic is the possibility of providing an endless food supply for the penned-in fish. The basic food of the sea is the microscopic organisms called plankton, which multiply like magic when conditions are just right. A plankton bloom occurs when minerals such as phosphorus and nitrogen are swept up from the depths into warmer, shallow water. Vegetable plankton, called phytoplankton, thrive on minerals carried by these upwellings, and their numbers increase fantastically. Zoo plankton are the tiny animals which thrive on phytoplankton and they also multiply phenomenally on the appearance of a source of food. In turn, small fish depend upon plankton as a basic food supply, and their population is in direct proportion to the density of the plankton bloom.

Upwelling currents carrying life-giving minerals from the depths now depend upon the uncontrolled whimsies of nature. Ocean currents perform in a way similar to the manner in which smoke dissipates inside a room. They may appear or disappear in any place, at any time. But man can change all this. Upwelling currents can be created artificially, and minerals can be directed to the area of controlled aquaculture. In this way an abundance of food will be assured to domesticated fish, and the enclosed area will support an astounding number.

Harvesting fish will also be revolutionized. Electric currents can be used to drive them into funnels where a suction tube will transport them to the processing area or cannery.

Plankton in itself can be utilized as food by men. Synthetic meats have been produced from it which, it is claimed, have a taste similar to steaks or roasts from prime beef. When this food resource is utilized, man need never again fear hunger and starvation.

The sea also contains power which future generations may utilize. This power may be obtained from the tremendous energy stored in wave action, tides, temperature differentials, and salinity differences. The extreme differences in temperature and salinity between the depths and the surface of the sea can be converted into electricity. Power for processing plants, equipment, and possibly undersea vehicles may be obtained directly from the sea itself. This could be extremely important in the development of industrial power in nations which now have no water power, and are deficient in coal, oil, and other heat-producing resources. Backward nations, held to primitive production methods by a lack of power, may witness an industrial revolution and be introduced to the conveniences of modern civilization.

The oceans are also extremely important to future generations in their absorption of CO_2, the gas exhaled by animal life and produced by heavy industry. The increasing expansion of industry and mechanization of our way of life is producing greater and greater quantities of CO_2 which is affecting the atmosphere and gas mixtures of the air. Adding to the rapid contamination of our air supply is the depletion of our forests and open fields of green plant life which nature intended as the means of absorbing CO_2 and maintaining the desired balance. CO_2 in the air absorbs and retains heat from the sun and, as the concentration increases, it may cause drastic changes in the weather. One theory is that it is already causing the earth to warm up and is beginning to melt the polar ice caps. If all the water stored in this ice were to melt and run into the sea, it would raise the level of the oceans approximately 100 feet.

The sea is absorbing CO_2 at a rate not presently known, but some areas of the ocean contain more CO_2 than others. Experiments may discover a method of increasing this absorption and hold contamination of the atmosphere below a critical level.

The oceans have always been extremely important in military operations and, in past history, the nation which controlled the sea dominated the world. Introduction of atomic warfare has diverted military attention from the surface to the more protected area of the depths. Submarine operations of the near future may decide the survival of great nations. All sea transport and cargo may be conducted underwater by both military and civilian steamship lines. In the serenity of deep water, free from the turbulence and danger created by surface storms and hurricanes, ocean liners can travel submerged to any port in the world under almost any conditions. Even icebound harbors would be open to submersible craft. They would travel to their destination beneath the ice, and surface at docks and piers in open water. Methods of water manipulation have already been developed which can maintain ice-free harbors and docks during any kind of weather. The process is simple and inexpensive. Only surface water becomes cold enough to freeze. Small pumps stationed on the bottom circulate warm water from the depths up to the surface and maintain the water temperature above freezing. Piers, harbors, and docks can be maintained ice free the year round through this simple method.

The increasing danger of radiation from fall-out of atomic warfare may force entire populations to exist in the safety of deep water. In the future, entire cities may be constructed in the depths. They would be self-contained, taking power, oxygen, minerals, food, and water from the sea. But little is known of the extent of radiation effects in the vastness of the oceans and how far its poison is carried by plankton, sea creatures, and currents. Experiments demonstrate that sea life in ten feet of water is temporarily safe, and in deeper water the protection may extend indefinitely.

For skin divers the most exciting prospects lie in the fields of subsea mining, salvage, and treasure hunting. An abundance of rare minerals exist on the sea floor awaiting development of equipment and techniques for their extraction. Cobalt, iron, copper, nickel, lead, and gold have been discovered in quantities that stagger the imagination. But present diving equipment is too primitive and inadequate for extensive work in deep water. We suffer from deep water sickness due to poisoning by nitrogen and carbon dioxide absorbed into our bodies, and we must spend so much time in decompression that our stay on the bottom is ridiculously short. Skin diving cylinders at present will withstand only a little over 2,000

172

pounds of pressure and last only 15 minutes at 100 feet. Future cylinders will be charged with liquid air or oxygen and helium at pressures in excess of 50,000 pounds. A cylinder the same size as those used at present, but charged with liquid air, would last 29 hours underwater under average diving conditions. This would give a diver the time needed to work at great depths. Breathing mixtures are also being studied which will reduce the hazard of the bends and nitrogen narcosis. Skin divers of the future will carry two tanks on their back, one charged with helium or hydrogen, and the other with oxygen. Special regulators will adjust the breathing mixture to the proper percentage according to the depth, and skin divers will be capable of working for extended periods at fantastic depths. Probably future salvage operations will be conducted as deep as the continental shelf which extends underwater away from shore to the edge of the abyss, reaching depths of 600 feet.

A spare cylinder of small size with a jet nozzle at its base and charged with liquid air may provide a means of jet propulsion for future skin divers. This same cylinder, or a lead from a main supply tank, could provide tremendous power for an underwater weapon so formidable a shot could stop a whale.

Through a system of aquaculture, underwater mines, farms, and fish husbandry will be practiced beneath the surface. Salvage crews and mining divers will operate from a submerged base, unaffected by surface storms and turbulence. In the tranquillity of the depths, submerged operations could continue uninterrupted even though a hurricane were raging above.

Diving vessels, similar to the bathyscaph, which are self-contained, and which maintain atmospheric pressure in the depths, will be used as a salvage base. Divers will emerge from compression chambers for their work periods and return to decompression chambers equipped with all the comforts of a private club. Decompression under these conditions will be a matter of days instead of hours, permitting longer exposure at great depths. Divers will operate underwater cranes, power shovels, and tractors which may be self-contained or not, depending on their use. Hand tools may either be powered by electricity or by small cylinders of liquid air.

Small submobiles will be used for running errands to and from the surface, maintaining supplies, and general supervision. And future generations may find sport and travel beneath the surface of the sea in submobiles of as many shapes and sizes as now exist in surface craft.

These are prospects for the future which offer exciting opportunities for skin divers interested in an underwater career. The possibilities are as vast and endless as the sea itself. Skin diving pioneers with imagination and ingenuity may unlock secrets of the sea, perform a great service to humanity and, in the process, gain prestige and fortunes for themselves.

At present the United States can boast of only 600 oceanographers, far too few to even think of making the necessary preliminary explorations for an under-sea program. This lack of trained personnel and the obsolete equipment they are forced to work with is causing America to lose the race into the sea. Before we can begin to catch up with our competition we must have more skin divers trained in the sciences of the sea.

Appendix

NO DECOMPRESSION TIME AND DEPTH TABLE

The following table was set up for average conditions. Do not cut corners; always allow leeway to the safe side when using any diving table.

Remember: The rate of ascent, 25 feet per minute, is a decompression process. DO NOT EXCEED.

Depth (feet)	Time at Depth for No Decompression (min.) *
0– 30	No limit
30– 40	120
40– 50	78
50– 60	55
60– 70	43
70– 80	35
80– 90	30
90–100	25
100–110	20
110–120	18
120–130	15

* (1) It is imperative that the rate of ascent not exceed 25 feet per minute.
  (2) Times indicated at various depths are not to be exceeded in any 12-hour period.

NAVY STANDARD DECOMPRESSION TABLE
(Using Compressed Air)

Depth of Dive (Feet)	Time on Bottom (Minutes)	Stops (Feet and Minutes)									Sum of Times at Various Stops (Minutes)	Approximate Total Decompression Time (Minutes)
		Feet 90	Feet 80	Feet 70	Feet 60	Feet 50	Feet 40	Feet 30	Feet 20	Feet 10		
40	120									0	0	2
40	180									2	2	4
40	Opt.* 240									4	4	6
40	300									6	6	8
50	78									0	0	2
50	120									2	2	5
50	150									5	5	8
50	Opt.* 190									9	9	12
50	300									12	12	15
60	55									0	0	3
60	75									2	2	5
60	110									13	13	16
60	Opt.* 150								5	15	20	24
60	180								7	16	23	27
60	210								8	18	26	30
70	43									0	0	3
70	60									4	4	8
70	75									13	13	17
70	90								4	16	20	24
70	Opt.* 120								13	16	29	33
70	150								18	21	39	43
70	180								21	32	53	57
80	35									0	0	3
80	50									6	6	10
80	70								6	16	22	27
80	100								20	16	36	41
80	Opt.* 115								22	26	48	53
80	150			\					28	29	57	62
90	30									0	0	4
90	45									6	6	10
90	60								9	16	25	30
90	75								18	14	32	37
90	Opt.* 95							2	27	21	50	56
90	130							9	27	29	65	71
100	25									0	0	4
100	40									12	12	17
100	60								18	16	34	39
100	75								27	21	48	53
100	Opt.* 85							6	28	21	55	61
100	90							8	27	24	59	65
100	120							17	28	48	93	99
110	20									0	0	5
110	35									12	12	17
110	55								22	21	43	49
110	Opt.* 75							14	27	37	78	84
110	105						2	22	29	50	103	110

*These are the optimum exposure times for each depth which represent the best balance between length of work period and amount of useful work for the average diver. Exposure beyond these times is permitted only under special conditions.

NAVY STANDARD DECOMPRESSION TABLE
(Using Compressed Air)

Depth of Dive (Feet)	Time on Bottom (Minutes)	Stops (Feet and Minutes)									Sum of Times at Various Stops (Minutes)	Approximate Total Decompression Time (Minutes)
		Feet 90	Feet 80	Feet 70	Feet 60	Feet 50	Feet 40	Feet 30	Feet 20	Feet 10		
120	18										0	5
120	30									11	11	17
120	45								18	21	39	45
120	Opt.* 65							13	28	32	73	80
120	100						5	22	27	69	123	130
130	15										0	5
130	35								11	15	26	32
130	52							6	28	28	62	69
130	Opt.* 60							13	28	28	69	76
130	90						9	22	28	69	128	136
140	15									4	4	10
140	30								8	21	29	36
140	45							5	27	27	59	67
140	Opt.* 55							15	28	32	75	82
140	85						14	22	32	69	137	145
150	15									7	7	14
150	30							13	21		34	41
150	38								28	30	58	65
150	Opt.* 50							16	28	32	76	84
150	80						18	23	32	69	141	150
160	15									9	9	16
160	34								27	28	55	63
160	Opt.* 45							17	28	43	88	96
160	75					3	19	23	34	68	147	156
170	15									11	11	18
170	30								24	27	51	59
170	Opt.* 40							19	28	46	93	102
170	75					9	19	23	38	68	157	167
185	15									25	25	33
185	26								24	37	61	70
185	Opt.* 35							19	28	46	93	102
185	65				18	18	23	37	65	51	212	223
200	15									32	32	41
200	23								23	37	60	69
200	Opt.* 40							22	18	44	84	106
200	60			5	18	18	23	37	65	51	217	229
210	15									35	35	44
210	Opt.* 30						5	16	28	40	89	100
210	55			6	18	18	23	37	65	51	218	231
225	15								6	35	41	51
225	Opt.* 27						22	26	35	48	131	143
225	60			13	18	18	23	47	65	83	267	280
250	15								17	37	54	66
250	Opt.* 25					2	23	26	35	51	137	150
250	50		12	14	17	19	29	49	65	83	288	303
300	12							20		37	57	70
300	Opt.* 20					9	23	26	35	51	144	159
300	45	6	14	15	17	18	31	49	65	83	298	315

*These are the optimum exposure times for each depth which represent the best balance between length of work period and amount of useful work for the average diver. Exposure beyond these times is permitted only under special conditions.

Recommended Reading

Abbott, R. Tucker: *American Seashells*. Princeton, Van Nostrand, 1954.

Barada, Bill: *Underwater Adventure*. Peterson Publishing, Hollywood, Calif., 1959.

Beebe, William: *Half Mile Down*. New York, Harcourt, Brace, 1934.

Beneath Tropic Seas. New York, Halcyon House, 1937.

Bigelow, Henry B.: *Oceanography*. New York, Harper.

Borghese, Prince Valerio: *Sea Devils*. Chicago, Regnery, 1954.

Carrier, Rick and Barbara: *Dive*. New York, Wilfred Funk, 1955.

Carson, Rachel: *The Sea Around Us*. New York, Oxford, 1951.

Cayford, John E.: *Underwater Work*. Cambridge, Md., Cornell Maritime Press, 1959.

Clark, Eugenie: *Lady with a Spear*. New York, Harper, 1953.

Coffman, F. L.: *Atlas of Treasure Maps*. New York, Nelson, 1957.

1001 Lost, Buried or Sunken Treasures. New York, Nelson, 1957.

Cousteau, J.-Y, and Frederic Dumas: *The Silent World*, New York, Harper, 1953.

Crile, Jane and Barney: *Treasure Diving Holidays*. New York, Viking, 1954.

Cross, E. R.: *Underwater Photography and Television*. New York, Exposition, 1955.

Davis, Sir Robert H.: *Deep Diving and Submarine Operations*. London, St. Catherine Press, 1936.

Diolé, Philippe: *The Undersea Adventure*. New York, Messner, 1953.

4000 Years Under The Sea. New York, Messner, 1954.

The Gates of the Sea. New York, Messner, 1955.

Ellsberg, Edward: *On the Bottom*. New York, Dodd, Mead, 1929.

Men Under the Sea. New York, Dodd, Mead, 1939.

Fisher, Ed L.: *Marine Tropicals*. New York, Crown, 1955.

179

Gilpatrick, Guy: *The Complete Goggler,* rev. ed. New York, Dodd, 1957.

Gorky, Bernard: *Mediterranean Hunter.* London, Souvenir Press, 1954.

Halstead, Bruce W.: *Dangerous Marine Animals.* Cambridge, Md., Cornell Maritime Press, 1958.

Hampton, T. A.: *The Master Diver and Underwater Sportsman.* New York, de Graff, 1956.

Hass, Hans: *Men and Sharks.* New York, Doubleday, 1954.
Diving to Adventure. New York, Doubleday, 1951.
Manta: Under the Red Sea with Spear and Camera. New York, Rand McNally, 1953.

Houot, Georges, and Piere Henri Willm: *2000 Fathoms Down.* New York, Dutton, 1955.

Isy-Schwart, Marcel: *Hunting Big Fish.* London, Burke.

Ivanovic, I. S.: *Spearfishing.* New York, Barnes, 1951.

Kuenen, Philip H.: *Marine Geology.* New York, Wiley, 1950.

Link, Marion Clayton: *Sea Diver.* New York, Rinehart, 1959.

Masters, David: *Deep Sea Diving.* London, Nelson.
Epics of Salvage. Boston, Little, Brown, 1954.

Midwinter, Roy: *Holidays Under the Sea.* London, JG. Fenn Ltd., 1958.

Norman, J. R., and F. C. Fraser: *Field Book of Giant Fishes.* New York, Putnam, 1949.

Owen, D. M.: *A Manual for Free Divers Using Compressed Air.* New York, Pergamon, 1955.

Potter, John S., Jr.: *Treasure Divers of Vigo Bay.* New York, Doubleday, 1958.

Quilici, Folco: *The Blue Continent.* New York, Rinehart, 1954.

Rebikoff, Dimitri: *Free Diving,* edited by Albert F. Van der Kogel. New York, Dutton, 1956.

Rebikoff, Dimitri, and Paul Cherney: *A Guide to Underwater Photography.* Philadelphia, Chilton, 1955.

Ricketts, Edward F., and Jack Calvin: *Between Pacific Tides,* rev. ed., Stanford, Stanford University Press, 1948.

Schenk, H. V., and H. W. Kendall: *Shallow Water Diving and Spearfishing.* Cambridge, Md., Cornell Maritime Press, 1954.
Underwater Photography, Cambridge, Md., Cornell Maritime Press, 1954.

Shepard, Francis P.: *The Earth Beneath the Sea.* Baltimore, Johns Hopkins Press, 1959.

Straughan, Robert P. L.: *Salt Water Aquarium in the Home.* New York, A. S. Barnes, 1959.

Taillez, Philippe: *To Hidden Depths.* New York, Dutton, 1954.

Tassos, John: *The Underwater World.* Englewood Cliffs, N.J., Prentice-Hall, 1957.

Thompson, Frank E., Jr.: *Diving, Cutting, and Welding.* Cambridge, Md., Cornell Maritime Press.

U.S. Naval Gun Factory, Experimental Diving Unit: *Diving with Self-Contained Apparatus* (Special Report Series 1954). Washington, D.C., U.S. Naval Gun Factory.

U.S. Navy Dept., Superintendent of Documents: *Navships 250–880—Bureau of Ships Diving Manual.* Washington, D.C., U.S. Government Printing Office, continuous as revised.

Van der Kogel, Albert, with Rex Lardner: *Underwater Sport.* New York, Holt, 1955.

Waldron, T. J., and J. Gleeson: *The Frogmen.* London, Evans, 1950.

Warren, C. E. T., and J. Benson: *Above Us the Waves.* London, Harrap, 1953.

Index

184

185

188

Lobsters—(*Continued*)
  clawed, 32–33, 105–106
  off Maine coast, 32–33, 105–106
  in Southern California, 107
  with spears, 107 (*See also* Spear-
    fishing)
Log jam, breaking of, 135–136
Logs, sunken, recovery of, 141–142
Long Beach breakwater, diving off,
  45
Long johns, 29, 30, 34
"Look-box," 149
Los Angeles, skin diving policemen
  in, 136–137
Lower California, geological discoveries in, 146–147
Lubricating oil, use of in compressors, 72
Lumber industry, loss of timber by,
  141–142

McCracken, Alex, 135–136
McCracken, Laurie, 135–136
Mae West, 103
Maine coast, lobster hunting off,
  32–33, 105–106
Manta rays, 122
Marine biology, 6, 43, 145
Marineland, California, 161
Maritime laws governing salvage,
  130
Marker buoy, 133–134 (*See also*
  Salvage operations)
Marx, Bob, 139–140
Masks, 10
  advantages of, 22, 25
  clearing of, 21–22, 68–71
  compensator, 21
  development of, 16, 21
  eye squeeze eliminated by, 21
  self-purging, 21
Massachusetts Council of Diving
  Clubs, 166
Mathison, Dr. Nelson, 139
Maverick, salvaging of, 144 (*See
  also* Salvage operations)
Mayas, water god of, 150
Meats, synthetic, production of
  from plankton, 170

Mediterranean Institute of Under-
  water Archaeology, 146
Medusa, 125–126
Men and Sharks, 55
Merrimack River, rescue operations
  in, 134–135
Metal detectors, 133 (*See also* Sal-
  vage operations)
Metals, corrosive properties of, 137,
  141
Mexican government, intervention
  of in treasure hunt, 139–140
Meyers, Jack, 117
Migratory game fish, 86, 94–95
Military operations, importance of
  sea in, 171–172
Milwaukee Public Museum, 145
Mineral oil, use of in compressors,
  72
Mining, underwater, 6, 144–145
  future, possibilities for, 172, 173
Monmouth, treasure hunt for, 139
Monterey coast, discovery of jade
  near, 141
  sharks off, 112, 115
  submarine gardens off, 31–32
Moray eels, 124–125, 161
Morgan, Henry, 138
Mosquito fish, 35
Motion pictures, underwater, 6, 67
  (*See also* Sea Hunt, film-
  ing of)
Mouthpiece, loss of, 69
Mussels, 86
  blue, 13
  recipes for cooking of, 107

Nantucket Island, sinking of
  Andrea Doria off, 33
Narcosis, nitrogen, 73, 76–80, 82,
  173
Nassau, 159
National Geographic Society, 138
Native pearl divers, 13–14
Natural resources, depletion of,
  168–169, 171
Nausea, causes of, 19, 20, 72
Navy Frogmen, 23, 30, 54

189

Shipwrecks, exploration of, 32, 33, 35, 62, 75–76, 146 (*See also* Salvage operations; Treasure hunting expeditions)

Shovels, power, underwater, 174

Siberia, skin diving in, 33

Siebe, Augustus, 52

Siebe Gorman and Company, 53

Silver, noncorrosive properties of, 137

Silver Shoals, Spanish galleons in, 138

Silver Springs, 159

Single hose units, 60–61 (*See also* Scuba)

Skin Diver magazine, 54, 63, 166

Skin diving operations, adventure in, 1–7, 145–146
  of American Indians, 47
  ancient, 10–13, 47
  in Arctic, 33, 40–43
  in cold water (*see* Cold water, effects of)
  conservation studies, 41–43, 145
  equipment for, basic, 8–26
    breathing (*see* Scuba)
  future, possibilities for, 168–174
    aquaculture, 173
    cities, underwater, construction of, 172
    fish husbandry and harvesting, 169, 170, 173
    in mining, 172, 173
    in salvage operations, 172–174
    subsea shipping, 171–172
    in treasure hunting, 172
  gun powder, discovery of, effect on, 13
  in ice water, 33–36
  mining, 6, 144–145, 172, 173
  motion pictures, 6, 67 (*See also Sea Hunt,* filming of)
  physical health, importance of in, 6–7, 14, 82–83, 158
  police investigations, 6, 136–137
  pollution studies, 145
  primitive, 13–14
  in Racine Quarry, 33–36

Skin diving operations—(*Cont.*)
  recommended reading for, 179–181
  recovery and search, 6, 36–37, 134–137
  rescue, 36–37, 134–136
  safety precautions for (*see* Safety precautions)
  salvage (*see* Salvage operations)
  scientific research, 6, 44, 145–147
  sea-otter studies, 41–43
  sources of information on, 7, 83–84
  spearfishing (*see* Spearfishing)
  treasure hunting (*see* Treasure hunting expeditions)
  in World War II, 13, 23, 30, 54

Sling guns, 98

Slip hitch, 65, 67–68

Slots, hazards in entering of, 88

Smith Lake, recovery of stolen safe from, 136

Smithson, Bill, 55

Smithsonian Institution, 138

Snorkel, 8, 10, 91–92, 95, 100, 103
  breathing with, 24–25, 46–47, 68, 104–105
  clearing of, 25
  selection of, 25

Sodom, discovery of ruins of, 145–146

Sonar depth finders, 133

Sound, rate of speed of, 113

South Pacific, native pearl divers in, 13–14

Southbridge Skin Divers Club, 166

Southern California lobsters, 107

Spanish galleons, sunken treasure in, 138, 140–141

Spearfishing, 15–16, 89–105
  bans against, 89, 90
  beginning of, 15–16
  breathing as factor in, 103–104
  championship, rules for, 103
  equipment for, break-away line, 95, 102–103
    inflatable float, 102–103
    parachute, 103

Water god of the Mayas, 150
Water power, obtaining of from sea, 170–171
Waterproofing agent, use of paraffin as, 30
Waves, cause and construction of, 87–88
Weight belts, 31, 34, 38–39
  drownings traced to, 38
  quick-release buckles on, 39, 67
  wearing of outside harness, 65, 68
Westwood, California, 62
Wet suits, 39–42
  Arctic research expanded by use of, 40–43
  buoyancy of, 40
  insulation with, 39–41
  leaks in, 40
  squeezes eliminated by, 39–40
Whale sharks, 122–123 (*See also* Sharks)
Whales, 4, 118–122
  acute senses of, 119–120
  baleen, 120, 122
  body heat of, maintenance of, 28–29

Whales—(*Continued*)
  breathing of, 24–25, 119
  echo-finding mechanism of, 119–120
  encounter with, 120
  killer, 120–122
  mouths of, 118
Whisky, recovery of from Great Lakes, 142
Women Ama divers of Japan, 14–15
Wood, corrosive properties of, 137, 141
Worcester Frogmen, 166
World War II, skin diving operations in, 13, 23, 30, 54
Wrestling championship, octopus, 117
Wright-Patterson Air Force Base, 129
Wrist seals, use of, 34, 37
Wyatt Earp, 165

Yucatán, lakes of, sacrifices in, 150
  sunken treasure ships off, 139–140